# Children's Liberation
## A BIBLICAL PERSPECTIVE

*Joseph Grassi*

THE LITURGICAL PRESS
Collegeville, Minnesota

Biblical quotations in this book are from The Holy Bible, Revised Standard Version, Catholic Edition.

Cover design by David Manahan, O.S.B.

1     2     3     4     5     6     7     8     9

**Library of Congress Cataloging-in-Publication Data**

Grassi, Joseph A.
    Children's liberation : a biblical perspective / Joseph A. Grassi,
      p.  cm.
    Includes bibliographical references.
    ISBN 0-8146-1964-9
    1. Children in the Bible.  I. Title.
    BS576.G73   1991                             91-6448
    220.8'30523—dc20                            CIP

# Contents

*Introduction*   5

**Part I Bless the Children! Children in Ancient
    Biblical Tradition**

Bless the Children! God's Greatest Gift   9

**Part II Children in the New Age**

1 Children as Successors of Jesus: Mark's Gospel   29

2 The Priority of Little Ones: Matthew's Gospel   56

3 The Children's Paradox and the Divine Child
    in Luke   72

4 Jesus' Beloved Youngster in John's Gospel   84

**Part III Epilogue: Finding the Divine Child**

Epilogue: Finding the Divine Child   113

*Notes*   123

*Bibliography*   126

*Selective Bibliography on Children*   128

# Introduction

*Children's liberation* is an expression rarely heard of or seen in print. Yet the word "gospel" means joyful good news of liberation for all, especially those who are "last or least." These last or least, even with all our modern progress, are still the little children. Even as I am writing, I recall my vivid impressions of a weekly public broadcasting television program I frequently watch entitled "The News Reported by Children." These young people report national and world events as seen and heard by young eyes and ears. Watching the programs, I have often been shocked by how little our legal system protects the rights of little ones from their birth until "legal age." The young reporters on this television series have investigated and reported story after story of the abuse of little children not only by their parents but by the society around them. Adults have ways to protect themselves and their rights, but children usually have neither the power to defend themselves nor anyone to stand up for them.

Our neglect of children even comes out in the scholarly study of Scripture. Relatively little has been written about children in the Bible, especially the primacy given to them in the message of Jesus. How are we to understand unusual expressions like those implying that to receive a child is to receive Jesus or the statement that the greatest of the disciples should be as the youngest? Why did Jesus choose a youngster as his beloved and favorite disciple in the Gospel of John? Why does

*To be accepting of ones own child-self is to be open & disposed to receive Jesus.*

*"search for St. T?" → End of the rainbow treasure —*

5

Luke's Gospel give so much attention to Jesus' birth and childhood?

This study, I feel, will present new insights into the meaning of Jesus' message and new hope for children's liberation. As we live in the concluding decade of this millennium, we need refreshing, new images for the future as we approach the year 2000. We all hope that the new millennium will somehow be a great age of renewal. Yet this can happen only through a rediscovery of the value and place of children. Here I refer not only to children in the outside world, but also to the neglected and forgotten child within each one of us.

*absolutely!*

A new age, of course, can only begin through a fresh intervention of the Spirit of God. How will this be recognized? One of the most beautiful images in the biblical prophets is found in Zechariah as he echoes God's promise, ''I will return to Zion, and will dwell in the midst of Jerusalem, and Jerusalem shall be called the faithful city, and the mountain of the LORD of hosts, the holy mountain.'' The sign of this divine return is a vista of abandoned thoroughfares transformed into busy streets not clogged with business traffic but with children playing in them: ''The streets of the city shall be full of boys and girls playing in them'' (Zech 8:5). God's return and presence is signaled by the joyful play of children.

We ask the readers of this book to identify with these children, participate in their play, and thus become younger each day. Picasso said, *''It takes a long time to become young.''*

Part I

# Bless the Children!
# Children in Ancient
# Biblical Tradition

# Bless the Children!
# God's Greatest Gift

And Abram said, "O Lord GOD, what will you give me, for I continue childless, and the heir of my house is Eliezer of Damascus. . . .you have given me no offspring and a slave born in my house will be my heir" (Gen 15:2-3).

The above words were Abraham's response to God who had just promised him an "exceedingly great reward" (Gen 15:1) for his courageous rescue of his nephew who had been taken captive by four kings. Yet no material reward could possibly take away Abraham's sadness at not receiving life's greatest gift, that of children. Children are the incarnation of the central biblical teaching that God is the root and source of all life. The gift of children in new life is an intimate share in his very nature.

God then took Abraham outside into the dark night, told him to look up at the stars and said, "Look toward heaven and number the stars, if you are able to number them; so shall your descendants be" (Gen 15:5). Despite Abraham's extreme old age and that of his wife, he believed God's words: "He believed the LORD; and he reckoned it to him as righteousness" (Gen 15:6). Only the blessing of children could enable Abraham to fulfill the role God had given him in history—to be a source of blessing to the whole world: "I will bless you, and make you great, so that you will be a blessing. . . . By you all the families of the earth shall bless themselves" (Gen 2-3).

9

This primacy of the gift of children is found in the very first pages of the Bible. The greatest privilege of human beings will be a share in God's own power to bring forth new life on earth. The Bible describes this in the final blessing God gives man and woman at the climax of the creation process:

> Male and female he created them. And God blessed them, and God said to them, ''Be fruitful and multiply and fill the earth and subdue it; and have dominion over the fish of the sea and over the birds of the air, and over every living thing that moves upon the earth'' (Gen 1:27-28).

The meaning of the first woman's name highlights this primacy of life-giving and life-bearing: ''The man called his wife's name Eve, because she was the mother of all living'' (Gen 3:20). Although God closed the gates of paradise because of the first parents' transgression, he opened up new hope for the future by this gift of new life to Adam and Eve: ''Adam knew Eve his wife, and she conceived and bore Cain, saying, 'I have gotten a child with the help of the LORD.' And again she bore his brother Abel'' (Gen 4:1-2).

In view of this primacy of the gift of children, the favorite image of a happy home was that of father, mother, and numerous children around a table at meals. The psalmist sings the praises of a man so blessed by God:

> Your wife will be like a fruitful vine within your house; your children will be like olive shoots around your table. Lo, thus shall the man be blessed who fears the LORD (Ps 128:3-4).

God's most precious reward and inheritance are children: ''Lo children are a heritage from the LORD, the fruit of the womb is a reward'' (Ps 127:3).

While the birth of any child was considered a divine blessing, exceptionally difficult births were regarded as extraordinary signs. Abraham and his wife Sarah were both very advanced in age when God promised them a son. It was so unbelievable that Abraham could not refrain from laughing when told the news:

> Then Abraham fell on his face and laughed, and said to himself, "Shall a child be born to a man who is a hundred years old? Shall Sarah, who is ninety years old, bear a child?" (Gen 17:17).

Sarah also laughed when she later overheard angels announce to Abraham that they would have a child in the coming spring (Gen 18:12). Consequently, when the promised child was born, Sarah exclaimed, "God has made laughter for me; everyone who hears will laugh over me" (Gen 21:6). Because of their laughter and surprise—before and after—the parents named their child *Isaac,* from the root meaning "laughter."

The continued birth of children was not only the greatest blessing for parents but also a sign of God's favor and his covenant with the whole nation of Israel. When Moses renewed the covenant with the whole people before entering the Promised Land, he and the Levites pronounced a blessing over Israel from the top of Mount Gerazim. This blessing enumerated all the future rewards for faithfulness to the covenant, and the greatest one was new life and fertility: "Blessed shall you be in the city, and blessed shall you be in the field. Blessed shall be the fruit of your body, and the fruit of your ground, and the fruit of your beasts, the increase of your cattle and the young of your flock" (Deut 28:3-4). At the end of his life, Jacob pronounced a seven-fold blessing on his favorite son Joseph beginning with the words, "God Almighty who will bless you with blessings of heaven above, blessings of the deep that crouches beneath, blessings of the breasts and of the womb" (Gen 49:25).

God required that the divine origin of this precious gift of life be especially recognized by the consecration of all first-born to him: "All that opens the womb is mine, all your male cattle, the firstlings of cow and sheep" (Exod 34:19). Then the parents or owners would symbolically buy them back with a special offering. In regard to children, the law stated, ''All the first-born of your sons you shall redeem'' (Exod 34:20).

The unique importance of children was enhanced by the fact that the ancients had a keen sense of living on through their children. In fact, this seems to have been the earliest understanding of immortality. Even casual observation showed them that identical features of parents and relatives were passed on to their offspring. This indicated that life itself was continuous and indestructible. Death did not mean obliteration but a transition into a new existence in their children.

This belief was connected to the power attached to personal names. Children carried on the *name* of their parents and in this sense made them live on. The greatest fear of the ancient Hebrews was that their names would be cut off or no longer remembered either by not having descendants or by the tragic deaths of children. The worst curse that could be uttered was, ''May your name be blotted out.'' The greatest blessing was that people's names be always remembered through their descendants and those who came after them. No wonder the word ''name'' is found some 850 times in the Hebrew Bible. A name stood for the presence and power of the person. This was especially true of the divine name. When Jacob blessed his son Joseph and his grandchildren, he prayed, ''In them [the children] let my name be perpetuated and the name of my fathers Abraham and Isaac; and let them grow into a multitude in the midst of the earth'' (Gen 48:16).

Sirach has left behind a precious testimony of this conviction that parents live on through their children, although his text refers especially to parents' example: ''The father may die, and yet he is not dead, for he has left behind him one like himself; while alive he saw and rejoiced, and when he died he was not grieved. He has left behind him an avenger against his enemies, and one to repay the kindness of his friends'' (Sir 30:4-5).

another way of saying you cannot enter eternal life except via your child-self

*Bless the Children! God's Greatest Gift* 13

In view of this importance of living on through children, some special provision had to be made for those who were childless. In this case, the line could be continued through the nearest relative. This was the purpose of the Levirate law (Deut 25:5-10). The law provided that if a married man died childless, his brother (or next of kin) should marry his brother's wife and the first child should bear the name of his brother "so that his name may not be blotted out of Israel" (Deut 25:6). It was the surviving brother's duty to "perpetuate his brother's name" (Deut 25:7).

Because of the sacredness of life in children and the Levirate obligation to carry on the family name, we can understand why the Scriptures regard the sin of Onan as so horrible that it resulted in his death. Onan was the second son of Judah, the son and successor of Jacob. The first son of Judah was Er who had married and then died without offspring. Consequently, Judah told his son Onan, "Go in to your brother's wife, and perform the duty of a brother-in-law to her, and raise up off-spring for your brother" (Gen 38:8). Onan pretended to do so, but the Bible text notes that "when he went in to his brother's wife, he spilled the semen on the ground, lest he should give offspring to his brother" (Gen 38:9). Consequently, his subsequent untimely death was regarded as a direct punishment from God.

Because of this central importance of children, biblical tradition emphasizes their special place in worship, prayer, and ritual. The Passover ritual in Exodus 13:8 reads, "You shall tell your son on that day, 'It is because of what the Lord did for me when I came out of Egypt.'" Also, when first-born animals were offered to God, an explanation was to be given to the children: "And when in time to come your son asks you, 'What does this mean?' you shall say to him, 'By strength of hand the Lord brought us out of Egypt, from the house of bondage'" (Exod 13:14).

The principal Hebrew prayer was the *Shemah*, because it was believed to have been composed and prescribed by God himself: "Hear O Israel, the Lord our God is one LORD, and you shall love the LORD your God with all your heart, and with all your soul, and with all your might" (Deut 6:4-5). Parents were to teach this prayer to their children so they could repeat it together at home and make it part of their daily life. God said through Moses, "You shall teach them [these words] diligently to your children, and shall talk of them when you sit in your house, and when you walk by the way, and when you lie down and when you rise" (Deut 6:7). The people's experience of God was to be a living tradition to be passed on to children and shared from generation to generation: "Keep your soul diligently, lest you forget the things which your eyes have seen, and lest they depart from your heart all the days of your life; make them known to your children and your children's children" (Deut 4:9).

## The Blessing of Children in Judaism

Judaism carried on the biblical tradition about the precious place of children. One of the most beautiful customs was that of blessing children. We have prominent examples in the first-century Gospels where Jesus blesses the children (Mark 10:16; Matt 19:13; Luke 18:15; we will have much to say about this in the coming chapters). Later Judaism followed the early biblical models of children's blessings. For example, Noah blessed his sons Shem and Japheth (Gen 9:26-27); Isaac blessed his sons Jacob and Esau (Gen 27; 28:1-4); Jacob blessed each of his children before his death (Gen 49). He also blessed his grandchildren, Ephraim and Manasseh (Gen 48). This last blessing is described in great detail, for it was also an adoption of these two children as his own. Jacob took the two chil-

*Handwritten margin notes: "confirms children represented LIFE"*

dren in his arms and kissed them. Then he placed his hands on the head of each one in turn and pronounced this blessing:

> The God before whom my fathers Abraham and Isaac walked, the God who has led me all my lifelong to this day, the angel who has redeemed me from all evil, bless the lads; and in them let my name be perpetuated, and the name of my fathers Abraham and Isaac; and let them grow into a multitude in the midst of the earth (Gen 48:15-16).

*Handwritten margin notes: "The 'name' was powerful enough to override lack of biological connection"*

It is striking to note once again in this text the strong conviction that parents live on in their children. Jacob mentions his father and grandfather whose names along with his own will be perpetuated in the children. The importance of the parental blessing is also found in Sirach: "A father's blessing strengthens the houses of the children, but a mother's curse uproots their foundations" (3:9).

In Judaism through the centuries, the custom of blessing children followed these ancient biblical models. The parental blessing of children is performed on Friday evening after sunset when the Sabbath begins. It is also done on the eves of the great holy days, on the Day of Atonement, and before leaving on a journey. This blessing is usually given by the father and sometimes by the mother also. It is given both to young children and adult children. For a boy, the blessing is modeled on that of Jacob for his grandsons with the words, "May God make you like Ephraim and Manasseh" (Gen 48:20). For a girl, the blessing follows that of the biblical Ruth: "May God make you like Sarah, Rebekah, Rachel and Leah" (Ruth 4:11). For both boys and girls, this is followed by the priestly blessing:

> The LORD bless you and keep you;
> The LORD make his face to shine upon you, and be gracious to you;
> The LORD lift up his countenance upon you, and give you peace (Num 6:24-26).

The parental blessing is also given before the marriage of a child and is especially important, as in the Bible, on the parents' deathbed. As long as grandparents are alive, their blessing is also especially prized.

## God's Greatest Gift and Human Weakness

*why?!*

Despite the many beautiful passages in the bible about children as the supreme gift of God, human weakness often caused them to be treated as the very least in human society, little above slaves. In practice it was the aged who received the most attention and respect in ancient times. In the popular view, wisdom was acquired through long human experience and was the special pride of older people. The Book of Proverbs describes gray hair as a crown of glory: "A hoary head is a crown of glory; it is gained in a righteous life" (16:31). Job declares, "Wisdom is with the aged, and understanding in length of days" (12:12). The same feeling is echoed by Sirach:

*The old folks coveted the "power"*

> What an attractive thing is judgment in grey-haired men, and for the aged to possess good counsel! How attractive is wisdom in the aged, and understanding and counsel in honorable men! Rich experience is the crown of the aged, and their boast is the fear of the Lord (25:4-6).

For a child, the highest virtue was to obey, reverence, and respect one's parents. To do so was to directly serve God himself. God's fourth commandment given at Mt. Sinai declared, "Honor your father and your mother." It was the only commandment that had a direct reward from God attached to it: "that your days may be long in the land which the LORD your God gives you" (Exod 20:12). Sirach expands on God's special blessing for children who actually obey God by obeying and honoring their parents:

> For the Lord honored the father above the children, and he confirmed the right of the mother over her sons. Whoever honors

his father atones for sins, and whoever glorifies his mother is like one who lays up treasure. Whoever honors his father will be gladdened by his own children, and when he prays he will be heard. Whoever glorifies his father will have long life, and whoever obeys the Lord will refresh his mother; he will serve his parents as his masters. Honor your father by word and deed, that a blessing from him may come upon you. For a father's blessing strengthens the houses of the children, but a mother's curse uproots their foundations (3:2-9).

Consequently, in ancient society, parents had almost absolute authority and power over their children. This had great repercussions both on the methods chosen to train children in virtue and on the traditions of society. The method involved absolute obedience to one's parents as representing not only God but civil authority and was understandable in view of the whole system of authority structures in the ancient world. However, the way it was often exercised can only be termed child abuse, since it was violently enforced by severe physical punishment often encouraged in biblical writings.

Everyone has heard the familiar proverb, "Spare the rod and spoil the child." The saying goes back many thousands of years, not only to the Bible but to other ancient literature. Examples from the Bible include the following: "He who spares the rod hates his son, but he who loves him is diligent to discipline him" (Prov 13:24); "Discipline your son while there is hope; do not set your heart on his destruction" (Prov 19:18); "Folly is bound up in the heart of a child, but the rod of discipline drives it far from him" (Prov 22:15); "Do not withhold discipline from a child; if you beat him with a rod, he will not die" (Prov 23:13); "He who loves his son will whip him often, in order that he may rejoice at the way he turns out" (Sir 30:1); and "Bow down his neck in his youth and beat his sides while he is young lest he become stubborn and disobey you" (Sir 30:12).

Biblical laws (which were civil as well as religious) supported the almost absolute rights of parents. The Book of Deuteronomy actually has a death penalty for the "stubborn and rebellious son":

> If a man has a stubborn and rebellious son, who will not obey the voice of his father or the voice of his mother, and, though they chastise him, will not give heed to them, then his father and his mother shall take hold of him and bring him out to the elders of his city at the gate of the place where he lives, and they shall say to the elders of his city, "This our son is stubborn and rebellious, he will not obey our voice; he is a glutton and a drunkard." Then all the men of the city shall stone him to death with stones; so you shall purge the evil from your midst, and all Israel shall hear and fear (21:18-21).

The same death penalty applied to children who cursed their parents: "He who curses his father or his mother shall be put to death" (Exod 21:17; Lev 20:9). However, no similar punishment was ordered for parents who offended their children and would certainly be old enough to know better. The father's rights, sanctioned by law, went even as far as the right to sell a daughter: "When a man sells his daughter as a slave, she shall not go out as the male slaves do" (Exod 21:7). The prejudice of the law in favor of males is blatant, since nowhere does the law allow a son to be sold.

Our reader may ask why we recall these examples of ancient laws to readers in our modern, enlightened age. First of all, there are unfortunately many Christians who still physically beat their children and justify their behavior from the biblical "models." Anne Eggebroten,[1] a mother and writer, first tried to follow teachers who appealed to the Bible for their approach to child discipline. She quotes James Dobson,[2] a very popular author of Christian books on children's discipline, and speaker on many radio programs, who writes, "My purpose has been nothing more ambitious than to verbalize the Judeo-

Christian tradition regarding discipline of children and to apply those concepts to today's families."[3] Dobson, however, insists that spanking should only be used when there is open defiance and disobedience; then the child should be spanked with "sufficient magnitude to cause the child to cry genuinely."[4]

After rejecting the "biblical model" and consulting other educators such as Bruno Bettelheim, Mrs. Eggebroten changed her whole approach to her children and made the following observations: "It was clear to me that a nonviolent theory was working a lot better for me than the spanking theory. . . . Physical punishments tend to escalate. . . . Behavior didn't change. . . . I gradually realized that I was spanking in anger, releasing my own frustration. . . . Violence was only causing the violence in the family to escalate: Roz saw us hit and she learned to solve her problems by hitting. Soon Ellen was hitting back. . . . The definition of discipline as a continuous teaching process (as between Jesus and the disciples) was much more persuasive to me than the discipline-as-punishment school of thought. . . ."[5]

In studying the history of children's "education," Anne Eggebroten found that she and other parents were following the examples of centuries of history. She notes that the concept of childhood is a relatively new idea starting in the late seventeenth and early eighteenth centuries. Before that time, children were considered little adults who had to be controlled and brought into the work world as soon as possible. She notes the findings of the historian Lloyd de Mause in his book *The History of Childhood:* "The further back in history we went, the lower the level of child care we found, and the more likely children were to have been killed, abandoned, whipped, sexually abused, and terrorized by their caretakers."[6]

Our own country has been far behind in taking leadership in the matter of children's rights. The constitution makes no provision for them nor has there yet been an equal rights amendment for women. Our "founding fathers" left us with an even more severe heritage than the biblical one thousands of years before. Puritan law in Massachusetts allowed civil authorities to whip disobedient children. In fact, a law of 1648 specifically ordered execution in two situations: a consistently rebellious son fifteen years of age or older and for older children of either sex who struck or cursed a parent. While we pride ourselves on scientific and technological progress, it is only in recent years that more and more cases of child abuse, previously carefully hidden, have come to light. The weekly news program reported by children on Public Broadcasting is an amazing eye opener on this hidden virus in what appears to be a modern, progressive society.

## Messages of Hope from Biblical Tradition

Fortunately, biblical tradition also presents remarkable rays of hope that counteract the black picture that weak human beings have created. The first area is that of the wisdom tradition. Here we find a central teaching that true wisdom is essentially a gift from God. It can be granted even to a child; it is not simply ingrafted through obedience to parents. The Book of Proverbs admits this: "For the Lord gives widsom; from his mouth come knowledge and understanding; he stores up sound wisdom for the upright" (2:6-7).

As an example, the wisdom of the young Joseph in governing Egypt is attributed to the Spirit of God. Pharaoh says, "Since God has shown you all this, there is none so discreet and wise as you are" (Gen 41:39). When the young King Solomon exhibits extraordinary wisdom in judging a difficult case, the biblical writer declares, "They [all Israel] stood in awe of the king, because they perceived that the wisdom of God was in him, to render justice" (1 Kings 3:28).

This wisdom was not considered hidden far off somewhere in space but God's own presence in nature and in history. Wisdom is so close to God that Proverbs describes it as a personification of God himself. Wisdom speaks of itself in these terms, "The LORD created me at the beginning of his work, the first of his acts of old" (Pro 8:22). Wisdom is like a companion of God present with him during the creation of the universe who continues to speak to human beings during their life. Those who listen find a new depth of life they had not previously understood: "Happy is the one who listens to me, watching daily at my gates, waiting beside my doors. The one who finds me finds life and obtains favor from the LORD" (Pro 8:34-35).

God's presence in nature is so evident that children immediately perceive it. When the Psalmist contemplates the heavens, the stars, and the sun, he sings with joy and children sing with him, "O Lord our Lord, how majestic is thy name in all the earth! Thou whose glory above the heavens is chanted by the mouth of babes and infants" (Psalm 8:1-2). Because wisdom is a gift from God, it can be found in children and little ones and can be granted to those who ask for it. King Solomon as a young man prayed for wisdom to guide him as the leader of his people. The First Book of Kings tells how King Solomon dreamed that God appeared to him and said, "Ask what I shall give you." The king replied, "Give your servant an understanding mind to govern your people that I may discern between good and evil; for who is able to govern this your great people" (3:5-9). The words in Hebrew are literally, "Give to your servant a *listening heart.*"

Following this story, an example of this God-given wisdom shows Solomon's extraordinary ability to judge difficult cases. The fame of his wisdom spread even to foreign countries occasioning the visit of the legendary Queen of Sheba (1 Kings 10). His "listening heart" made him open to all the wonders of nature and the universe: "He spoke of trees, from the cedar that is in Lebanon to the hyssop that grows out of the wall; he spoke also of beasts, and birds, and of reptiles, and of fish. And people came from all nations to hear the wisdom of Solomon, and from all the kings of the earth, who had heard of his wisdom" (1 Kings 5:13-14).

God's gift of wisdom to Solomon is described in a poetic manner in the Book of Wisdom. The king acknowledges that his birth is completely human like that of any other child:

> When I was born, I began to breathe the common air, and fell upon the kindred earth, and my first sound was a cry like that of all. I was nursed with care in swaddling cloths. For no king has had a different beginning of existence; there is for all mankind one entrance into life, and a common departure (7:3-6).

However, the gift of God's wisdom came to him through prayer and completely transformed him: "I prayed and understanding was given me; I called upon God, and the spirit of Wisdom came to me" (Wis 7:7).

This wisdom became the most precious possession of the young king. He describes wisdom as more beautiful than the sun, excelling every constellation of the stars (Wis 7:29). The king dedicated himself to the search for wisdom and described it with imagery befitting the quest for an inner bride: "I loved her and sought her from my youth, and I desired to take her for my bride, and I became enamored of her beauty" (Wis 8:2). The king is certain that only wisdom can transform his life: "I determined to take her to live with me, knowing that she would give me good counsel and encouragement in cares and grief. Because of her I shall have glory among the multitudes and honor in the presence of the elders, though I am young" (Wis 8:9-10).

A second area of hope connected with children is the expected birth of a future child of the dynasty of David. At a time when the existence of David's line was threatened by a coalition of kings about to besiege Jerusalem, Isaiah had a vision of a new child being born to the king. This was in effect a guarantee that the nation would continue to exist. God said to the prophet, "Behold the Lord himself will give you a sign. Behold, a young woman shall conceive and bear a son, and shall call his name Immanuel" (Is 7:14). The child is to be called by this name which means "God is with us" because the very existence of the child is a sign that God is with his people keeping his promises.

The image of this future child was constantly before the prophet who simply refers to him as THE CHILD. Referring to the near future God says to Isaiah, "Before THE CHILD knows how to refuse the evil and choose the good, the land before whose two kings you are in dread will be deserted" (Is 7:16). Further on Isaiah will declare,

> For to us a child is born, to us a son is given; and the government will be upon his shoulder and his name will be called "Wonderful Counselor, Mighty God, Everlasting Father, Prince of Peace." Of the increase of his government and of peace there will be no end, upon the throne of David, and over the kingdom to establish it, and to uphold it with justice and with righteousness from this time forth and for evermore. (9:6)

The idyllic image of a return to the childlike innocence of the Garden of Eden was connected with hopes for the new age and Messianic times which arose from the traditional picture of the end times as a return to the beginning of time. In the garden before the fall, the first parents had a certain childlike innocence about them. They had no clothes and were not even aware that they were naked (Gen 2:25). Even the wild animals were tame, and Adam could call them all by name (Gen 2:20). The animals were tame because they were imagined along with man and woman to be vegetarian, since God had allotted them only the fruits of the earth as their food (Gen 1:29-30).

Isaiah presents a beautiful picture of the restoration of paradise: animals who were traditional enemies graze side by side. Three times in Isaiah 11:6-9 the image of a little child is introduced:

> The wolf shall dwell with the lamb and the leopard shall lie down with the kid and the calf and the lion and the fatling together and a little child shall lead them. The cow and the bear shall feed; their young shall lie down together; and the lion shall eat straw like the ox. The sucking child shall play over the hole of the asp, and the weaned child shall put his hand on the adder's den. They shall not hurt or destroy in all my holy mountain; for the earth shall be full of the knowledge of the LORD as the waters cover the sea.

A third area of hope and surprise can be found in God's mysterious plans which upset human expectations and often work through weak human creatures and little ones. The ordinary path to success in the world is through power usually exercised by those who are older and endowed with authority, "wisdom," and experience. Yet we find in the Bible that God often turns the tables and works through the least likely people. On notable occasions, this means that he will work through those who are younger rather than older, through little ones and children rather than through great and powerful people.

A notable example of God's surprising reversals can be found in the opening pages of the Bible. When Adam and Eve have their first child, Eve exclaims with joy, "I have gotten a man with the help of the LORD" (Gen 4:1). It would be hard to imagine a person of more importance, power, and expectations than the first-born son of the biblical human race. However, the first parents soon had another, a younger son, and contrary to all human standards, God favors the younger more than the older. When both sons offered sacrifice, the Bible notes, "The LORD had regard for Abel and his offering, but for Cain and his offering he had no regard" (Gen 4:4-5).

Another example is found in the story of Jacob, the father of the people of Israel. By all rights, his elder brother, Esau, should have had that privilege, since he was the first one of the twins to be delivered. Yet even before their birth, God revealed his mysterious plans to their mother, Rebecca, in these words, "Two nations are in your womb, and two people, born of you, shall be divided; the one shall be stronger than the other, the elder shall serve the younger" (Gen 25:23).

The same pattern unfolds in the story of the family of Jacob. There, it is not his oldest sons who play the principal part in the biblical drama. Instead, it is his young son Joseph, who is only seventeen years old when God sends him dreams foreshadowing his extraordinary role in preserving his people from hunger and death. (Gen 37:1-11). Before Jacob dies, he gives Joseph, not his older sons, a double blessing that includes adopting Joseph's two sons, Manasseh and Ephraim, as his own (Gen 48:5). Even here, one of God's mysterious reversals take place. Joseph places his older son, Manasseh, at Jacob's right hand to receive the first and most important blessing, yet Jacob unpredictably crosses his hands and places his right hand over on the head of the younger son, Ephraim. Joseph tries to correct this by moving his father's hand, but Jacob refuses to do so stating that the youngest son will be the more important (Gen 48:17-19).

The most interesting example of all occurs in the story of David, the king of Israel, to whom God made a special promise that was the source of Messianic hope for the future. God instructed Samuel, the prophet, to go to Bethlehem to the family of Jesse and anoint a new king over Israel. Upon his arrival, Jesse and his seven older sons were at the home. On seeing Eliab, the oldest son, Samuel thought that surely this was the chosen one to be anointed, but the Lord said to Samuel, "Do not look on his appearance or on the height of his stature, because I have rejected him; for the LORD sees not as human beings see; they look on the outward appearance but the LORD looks upon the heart'' (1 Sam 16:7). After this, Jesse presented each of the other six sons in turn, but the same response came from God.

Finally, Samuel said to Jesse, ''Are all your sons here?'' And he answered, ''There is still the youngest, but behold he is keeping the sheep'' (1 Sam 16:11). Keeping sheep was usually the task of youngsters or children who were not strong enough for other work. Samuel told Jesse to send for David, this youngest son, and when he came Samuel anointed him to be the future king: ''Then Samuel took the horn of oil, and anointed him in the midst of his brothers; and the Spirit of the LORD came mightily upon David from that day forward'' (1 Sam 16:13). The same theme occurs in the famous battle between David and Goliath. David was still too young to go out to battle the Philistines, and his father had directed him to continue to take care of the sheep (1 Sam 17:14). King Saul was very hesitant when David offered to battle the Philistine giant, noting that he was only a youth. When Goliath saw the youngster coming to him armed with only a slingshot and stones, he despised him as being a mere child. Yet David trusted in God to give him the victory despite impossible odds (1 Sam 17:31-51).

So far, we have only examined the place of the child in the Old Testament. The remainder of this book will try to show how the Gospels build on these scriptural foundations and point the way to a true liberation of children by awarding them first place in the new age of God's promise. We limit our study to the Gospels because they contain the most information about this essential theme.

# Part II

# Children in the New Age

1

# Children as Successors of Jesus: Mark's Gospel

## Mark, the Gospel of Liberation

The situation in which Mark's audience lived[7] provides the key for understanding his message. The community listeners to his Gospel were under heavy pressure from abusive Roman authority and lived in fear of persecution. For relief, some Christians anxiously awaited Jesus' return as a powerful Messiah to liberate them from this Roman oppression. There are also signs that some community leaders had an excessively authoritarian view of their role in the community. An understanding of this atmosphere is essential for discovering why Mark gives such unusual attention to children in key parts of his Gospel.

First, let us look at the indications of outside pressures on community members from abusive Roman power.[8] These pressures greatly intensified after the Jewish War with Rome, 66–70 A.D. They had begun under Nero in the sixties and increased after the war because Jews were regarded as dangerous revolutionaries, and Christians could hardly be distinguished from the Jews, since they believed in a Jewish Messiah. Some Gospel texts refer explicitly to persecution. The parable of the seed describes those who ''have no root in themselves, but endure for a while; then, when tribulation or *persecution* arises on ac-

29

count of the word, immediately they fall away'' (4:17). Jesus promises James and John that they will drink of the same cup that he will and be baptised with the same baptism (10:39). In Jesus' last testament on The Mount of Olives, he predicts to his disciples that they will be hated, brought to trial before councils and kings, beaten in synagogues, and even betrayed by members of their own family (13:9, 12).

Implicit references to persecution can be found if the above direct statements are kept in mind. For example, Roman oppressors were quick to attribute the good works of Christians to the devil. So Jesus speaks of blasphemy against the Holy Spirit by those who attribute his good works or those of his disciples to the devil (3:28-30). The storm at sea with Jesus asleep in the boat would have symbolic meaning for people caught in the storms of persecution who might feel that Jesus was ''asleep'' and not really with them (4:35-41). The call to take up the cross and follow Jesus would be readily understood by those who faced the possibility of crucifixion themselves as followers of a revolutionary Messiah. Those who wavered were warned that for not confessing Jesus they would be shamed before others at the return of the Son of Man (8:34-38).

Yet there were Christian prophets and teachers with a considerable following who taught that these tribulations of early Christians were only temporary and that Jesus would soon return in great power to liberate them from Roman oppression. For these teachers, the destruction of the Temple in 70 A.D. was a sign from God that this powerful return was about to take place. Jesus warns his disciples against them: ''Many will come in my name, saying, 'I am he,' and lead many astray'' (13:6). Also he states, ''Then if anyone says to you, 'Look, here is the Christ!' or 'Look, there he is!' do not believe it. False Christs and false prophets will arise and show signs and wonders to lead astray, if possible, the elect'' (13:21-22).

This prediction of Jesus' imminent and powerful return was connected with a coming judgment and end of history. So it was necessary for Jesus to announce to his disciples that his return was not linked with the local, actual destruction of Jerusalem. In contrast, his return would have universal signs and effects: he would send his messengers out to gather his elect from the four ends of the earth (13:26-27). Unlike those teachers who were making definite time schedules and pointing to signs in history like earthquakes and wars, Jesus definitely states that no one will know the time of his return: "Of that day or that hour no one knows, not even the angels in heaven, nor the Son, but only the Father" (13:32).

With this in mind, Jesus tells the Gospel audience that they themselves will have an active part in determining the time of his return in triumph, since it will be accomplished through their own patience and willingness to even give up their lives for what they believe in, imitating Jesus. Only by this means will they bring about the conversion of the rest of the world, and then Jesus will return. So Jesus tells them to stand before governors and kings for his sake, as a witness (*martyrion*) to them. The Gospel must be preached to the whole world before he will return (13:10). This preaching will take place essentially through his followers' personal example and witness which will give new meaning to Christians' suffering and persecution: it will provide the necessary witness to the Gentiles and make possible their conversion so that the return of Jesus may come about.

Consequently, the Gospel attaches great importance to the response to this challenge. It must be a total response, even to the willingness to die for one's faith. Jesus says, "The one who endures to the end will be saved" (13:13). The introductory and concluding literary frame of Jesus' last testament in Mark 13 make this clear. The introduction is the story of the "widow's mite." Jesus praises the woman because she gave *everything* she had, even her whole life (12:44). At the conclusion of Jesus' last discourse we find the parallel story of the woman at Bethany. She poured a jar of precious ointment on Jesus' head. The disciples were indignant about this "waste." But Jesus praised her because, like the widow, she gave all she could (14:8). The example of her action, if followed by others, will influence the whole world, for Jesus solemnly announces, "Wherever the gospel is preached in the whole world, what she has done will be told in memory of her" (14:9).

In a similar vein, Mark narrates the story of Jesus' death as a model for Christians who are likewise faced with suffering and death for what they believe. Jesus was arrested and put on trial; he confessed who he was before the high priest. Then, he was condemned to death and crucified by Roman power and authority. He persevered until the end even though he was abandoned by his friends and disciples who all fled when he was arrested (14:50). Christians might have been tempted to believe they were abandoned by God when such things happened to them and cry out like Jesus, "My God, my God, why have you forsaken me" (15:34). They might hope that God through Elijah or one of the prophets would deliver them at this moment. Yet they had to be ready to be taunted like Jesus with the words, "Let us see whether Elijah will come to take him down" (15:36).

The abandoned and persecuted Christians in those black hours might well have wondered what value such a humiliating death had. Their only model was Jesus, the Gospel hero. Despite the shameful appearance of his death, he persevered until the end. His last breath, a loud confident cry, marked the death of a victorious hero and soon had dramatic effects. His hardened executioner, a Roman centurion skilled in crucifixions, was moved to conversion, received forgiveness from God, and cried out, "Truly this man was Son of God" (15:39). Christians who follow Jesus even to the cross will have the same effect on other Romans and be instruments of their conversion. They will make possible the necessary condition for Jesus' return (13:10): witnessing the Gospel to the Gentiles.

To prepare for the disciples' identification with Jesus in the supreme moments of his passion and death, Mark's Gospel has a planned sequence of dramatic narrative. In the beginning, Jesus is called to obedience and sonship with the Father when the heavens open at his baptism and God's voice announces to him, "You are my beloved son" (1:11). At the end of the Gospel, Jesus fulfills his role as the obedient son by dying on the cross. This is followed by a dramatic opening of the heavens symbolized by the tearing of the temple veil and the centurion's confession that Jesus is the Son of God (15:39). Jesus' disciples are called to participate in these events by his first words to them, "Follow me and I will make you become fishers of human beings" (1:17). These words summarize the Gospel, for if Jesus' disciples really follow him all the way, even to the cross, they will be able to cast out their nets and bring other "centurions" into the kingdom.

The way in which disciples can participate in Jesus' whole action is explained in a central part of the Gospel which contains three predictions of Jesus' suffering and death followed by three teaching sections on how the disciples must follow along the same way. Peter's confession introduces the first prediction-discipleship section. Jesus asks his disciples, "Who do you say that I am?" Peter responds, "You are the Christ" (8:30).

Jesus then commands his disciples to be silent for fear they have misunderstood the title Peter gave him in terms of temporal power. He then begins to teach them about his coming passion and death: "The Son of Man must suffer many things, and be rejected by the elders and the chief priests and the scribes, and be killed, and after three days rise again" (8:31). The word "must" implies obedience to a divine plan in the

Scriptures. Peter cannot accept this idea and earns a sharp rebuke from Jesus who states that he is following Satan's ways
by refusing to accept the cross (8:33). For the first time, Jesus
tells his disciples that they also must follow the same way, even
to the cross: "Those who wish to follow me must deny themselves, take up their cross and follow me; those who would
save their lives will lose them" (8:34).

Jesus' obedience to his Father is thus the disciple/audience's
way, also. But they will be obedient to God's voice as it comes
through Jesus. This saying is so difficult, so humanly impossible that a vision of the transfigured Jesus follows to confirm
it. The midpoint of Mark's Gospel resembles its beginning and
end where the heavens open and there is the announcement
that Jesus is the Son of God. The voice of the Father, "This
is my beloved Son," is now directed to the disciples who are
told, "listen to him," in regard to the hard saying about taking up the cross and following Jesus even to suffering and
death.

The parallel sequences for Jesus and the disciple are significant. For Jesus there will be suffering, death, and resurrection. For the disciple there will likewise be suffering (taking
up the cross) and death (losing one's life for his sake). For the
disciple, however, the third step will not be immediate resurrection but rather a special place at the return of Jesus. If anyone has been ashamed of his words, the Son of Man in turn
will be ashamed of *him* when he returns in glory with the angels. So the sequence for the disciple is suffering, death, and
the return of Jesus.

The second sequence builds on the first and expands it.
Jesus announces that he will be delivered up to the hands of
men (9:31), then die and rise again. At the end of this sequence,
in answer to Peter's question, Jesus responds that the disciple
who leaves family or home will have persecutions in this life
and eternal life in the age to come. Once again the sequence

is suffering, death, and the return of Jesus (seemingly indicated by the age to come).

The third sequence is even more explicit in regard to Jesus' sufferings: he will be delivered up to Gentiles and will be mocked, spit upon, and scourged before being killed (10:33-34). The story of James and John illustrates what Jesus expects of a disciple. These two disciples who are also brothers ask Jesus to let them sit, one at his right hand and the other at his left, in glory (10:35-45). Instead, Jesus tells them they must drink his cup and be baptized in suffering like his if they wish to be with him in glory. The picture is one of close imitation of the Master. The word "glory" makes us think of the return of Jesus where the same expression is used in the first prediction. The suffering and martyrdom of the disciples will lead to and make possible the parousia (the return or appearance of Jesus) by an intimate union of their sufferings with the suffering and death of Jesus with whom they have shared the same cup.

How the union of the sufferings of Jesus and his disciples will affect the Gentile world is not as clear here as in Jesus' last testament in chapter 13. However, it is implicit in the universal nature of Jesus' return which is for the whole world. In addition, it is probable that the concluding statement of the section brings this out: "The Son of Man also came not to be served but to serve, and to give his life as a ransom for many" (10:45). The word "many" has a universal implication in view of the audience's experience of the whole Gospel message.

In Mark's Gospel, then, the audience is not to hope for liberation from abusive Roman power through some great act of God like that of Jesus' return in glory and judgment. Their true liberation can only come in a non-violent way through imitation of Jesus. Like Jesus, they must be willing to suffer and die for what they believe in. Only their personal example can effectively change others and shorten the time before the much-longed-for return of Jesus.

*But the mother"*

There seems to be another important area, a misuse of liberation, that the Gospel author wishes to emphasize: the use of domination and control by community members. This was hinted at in the story of James and John, two chief apostles who are pushing for the first places in the kingdom. Their request also angers the other ten apostles. Jesus has to teach all of them that authority and power are not to be exercised as in the Gentile (Roman) world but through loving service where the greatest among them should be like the least, a servant (10:35). This same teaching occurs on another occasion when the Twelve were arguing among themselves while on a journey about who would be the greatest in the kingdom (9:33-35). In addition, the same theme occurs when Jesus tells John not to try to stop others who are healing and exorcizing demons in Jesus' name (9:38-41). All these stories about the apostles seem to be directed toward future leaders in Mark's audience.

However, who are the ones in the Gospel who actually follow Jesus all the way to the cross, and who are his real counterparts? One of the Twelve, Judas, betrayed him. Peter, his chief apostle and rock, denied three times that he knew Jesus. The rest of his disciples all fled when Jesus was arrested. The Gospel contains many surprises. Jesus is indeed the hero of the Gospel, but his real counterparts are those who follow him from the beginning to the end. In the beginning, in Galilee, Jesus had said, "Follow me and I will make you fishers of human beings" (1:17). However, at the cross, none of Jesus' male disciples are present in Mark's account. Instead, we find a group of women headed by Mary Magdalene who had followed Jesus all the way from Galilee. They are the ones who make possible the spread of the Gospel to the world because they follow the same path as Jesus. Mark has prepared the way for these heroes and counterparts of Jesus through the dramatic sequence of his Gospel. I have traced the spiritual journey of these women in another book entitled, *The Hidden Heroes of the Gospels: The Female Counterparts of Jesus*.[9]

But there is another great surprise in Mark's mystery drama. Children will appear as Jesus' true spiritual successors, even in contrast at times to Jesus' chosen Twelve, if we look carefully at this Gospel.

## Children's Liberation in Mark's Gospel

To prepare for this theme of children's liberation, Mark is anxious to provide examples of Jesus' special concern for children. Jesus' greatest miracle is the resurrection of the young daughter of Jairus. She seems to have been her parents' only hope of future descendants. In fact, Luke calls her the only daughter (8:42). She is twelve years old and of marriageable age. Jesus not only touches her and brings her back to life, but also enables life to continue on in the family of Jairus through the possibility of grandchildren. The same theme is central to the accompanying story of the woman with a continual flow of blood. She was perpetually unclean and could not marry or have children. Jesus heals and restores to her also the possibility of marriage and children.

Our main focus will be on the central place of children's stories in the three prediction/discipleship sections of Mark. The first one is like a resurrection story: A young boy has been afflicted with epileptic-like seizures all during his childhood that have often brought him to the point of death. It was so difficult a case that the remaining disciples who remained behind could work no cure while Jesus was on the Transfiguration Mountain. In desperation, the father's child appealed to Jesus for help: "If you can do anything, have pity on us and help us." Jesus in turn replied, "If you can! All things are possible to him who believes" (9:22-23). Following the father's touching appeal for the gift of faith, Jesus exorcised the boy's demon and the text relates that "After crying and convulsing him terribly, it came out, and the boy was like a corpse; so that most of them said, 'He is dead.' " (9:26)

This story has a strong resurrection motif and heightens the importance of the following triple emphasis on children in 9:33-10:16.

It is surprising how these important stories about children and Jesus have been neglected in scriptural studies.[10] To be sure, commentators have emphasized Jesus' compassion for little children or have argued whether the texts teach anything about the baptism of children in the early Church. However, little has been said about the central function of these stories in the whole context of the Gospel message. First of all, they form a literary frame for some of Jesus' most important teachings. At the beginning of the frame, Jesus uses the example of the child when the disciples were arguing over who would be the most important in the kingdom. The ending frame occurs when Jesus has the disciples bring the children to him comes after his difficult teaching about divorce which contrasts with that of the Pharisees and creates great difficulty for his disciples.

The first episode follows Jesus' second prediction about his coming passion and death. It also initiates the second section: The teaching about discipleship for Mark's community. As they listen to Jesus' telling his disciples he must suffer and die, their thoughts certainly turn to the question of succession to Jesus after his death. This is because he immediately brings up the matter of the disciples arguing along the way about who would be the greatest (naturally among themselves!) in the coming kingdom. Mark's text and its details will be important for us:

> He [Jesus] asked them, "What were you discussing on the way?" But they were silent; for on the way they had discussed with one another who was the greatest. And he sat down and called the Twelve; and he said to them, "If any one would be first he must be last of all and servant of all." And he took a

child, and put him in the midst of them; and taking him in his arms, he said to them, ''Whoever receives one such child in my name receives me; and whoever receives me, receives not me but him who sent me'' (9:33-37).

We note the following significant details in the text: there is a direct confrontation with the attitude of the *Twelve* who are all thinking about having places of power and authority. Jesus calls them, sits down formally as a teacher, and makes a very important statement. First he acts, placing a child in their midst as the most important person. Then he *takes the child into his arms.* The same expression is used in the closing story about children in 10:16. As we will see, the phrase has an important scriptural background as part of an ancient adoption ritual. Jesus takes a child as the image of his true successor and does not conform to the twelve apostles' expectations of power.

*wow!*

Jesus confirms his non-verbal teaching (through gesture) by a solemn word: ''Whoever receives one such child in my name receives me; and whoever receives me, receives not me but him who sent me.'' I use the word ''succession'' because the text literally says that receiving the child is the same as receiving Jesus himself, and thus receiving God. This meaning can be confirmed by its use in succession contexts in other Gospels. At the end of Jesus' mission instruction to the Twelve in Matthew 10, he concludes his teachings with the identical saying (10:40). The same words are also found in the Last Supper, last testament, and succession context of John chapter 13. After washing the disciples' feet and telling them they should follow his example, Jesus concludes with a solemn double amen statement: ''Truly, truly, I say to you, he who receives any one whom I send receives me; and he who receives me receives him who sent me'' (13:20).

Without a break in this scene, we have another example of contrast to the disciples' attitudes. John, one of the top apostles, said to Jesus, ''Teacher, we saw a man casting out

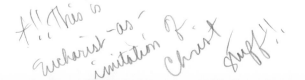

*+!! This is eucharist - as imitation of Christ stuff!!*

demons in your name, and we forbade him, because he was not following us'' (9:38). Jesus once again contradicts the disciple's exclusive attitude by stating, ''Do not forbid him; for no one who does a mighty work in my name will be able soon after to speak evil of me'' (9:39). Then, for a second time, Jesus refers to the child in their midst with the words, ''Whoever causes one of these little ones who believe in me to sin, it would be better for him if a great millstone were hung round his neck and he were thrown into the sea'' (9:42). This text clearly brings out the priority of little children in the disciples' teaching, particularly in contrast to John's exclusivism which would indeed be a scandal to children who are traditionally less exclusive in their relationships.

The third reference to children concludes the literary frame at a very significant point. Jesus has just confronted the Pharisees with a new, difficult teaching on divorce. His own disciples find it difficult and question the master privately in the house. There, Jesus has to repeat his teaching and make it even more explicit. Then, an important moment follows:

> And they were bringing children to him, that he might touch them; and the disciples rebuked them. But when Jesus saw it he was indignant, and said to them, ''Let the children come to me, do not hinder them; for to such belongs the kingdom of God. Truly, I say to you, whoever does not receive the kingdom of God like a child shall not enter it.'' And he took them in his arms and blessed them, laying his hands upon them'' (10:13-16).

In this story, we find the strongest confrontation between Jesus and the disciples. The latter rebuked the mothers who were bringing children to Jesus, implying that the Master had much more important matters to take care of. The text has considerable emotion behind it, recording that Jesus was visibly *indignant* and publicly contradicted his disciples by saying, ''Let the children come to me, do not hinder them; for to such be-

longs the kingdom of God'' (10:14). Children, in contrast to
the disciples' attitude, were not to be the least important
beneficiaries of the kingdom but the first actual owners of the
kingdom. To parallel the opening story, the expression ''receiving'' is brought in. Only this time it is a matter of imitating
children by receiving the kingdom as a child would—wholly
and without reserve as is its attitude toward a loving parent.

The final action of Jesus in blessing the children has great
significance in view of its context in the Gospel and its biblical
background. In Mark, it is in the context of a triple teaching
of Jesus about his death. In the same way, in the Bible, the
blessing of children had special importance before a person's
death. It was a transfer of power and authority to the child
who then became a true successor of the parent. Thus Isaac
blesses his two sons Jacob and Esau before his death (Gen 27);
Jacob in turn blesses each of his twelve children before he dies
(Gen 49).

Jesus' action in blessing fits into a definite ritual pattern for
a final blessing such as we find described in detail when Jacob
gives a special blessing to Joseph's two sons, Ephraim and
Manasseh, and adopts them as his own (Gen 48). Joseph *brings*
(48:10) the two boys to his aged father Jacob just as the parents were bringing the little children to Jesus. Jacob ''kissed
them and embraced them'' (48:10) just as Jesus took the children into his arms, although the action of kissing is not specifically mentioned by Mark. Jacob touched each one by placing
his hands on the head of each boy, just as Jesus laid his hands
on each of the children.

From these detailed similarities to the biblical ritual of blessing, Mark would have his audience understand that Jesus'
blessing of children made them his special successors. This is
the only blessing by Jesus recorded in Mark's Gospel. By way
of comparison, Luke attributes special significance to Jesus'
blessing by concluding his Gospel in this way, ''Then he [Jesus]

led them out as far as Bethany, and lifting up his hands he blessed them. While he blessed them, he parted from them, and was carried up into heaven" (24:50). This blessing seems to convey succession and continuity, since the Gospel then relates that the disciples returned to Jerusalem with great joy.

### Receiving the Kingdom "like a child" (Mark 10:15)

"Amen I say to you, whoever does not receive the kingdom of God like a child shall not enter it." This special Amen statement of Jesus alerts the audience to pay close attention to an important point. The preceding description of bringing children to him (10:13) is a response to hearing about Jesus that goes through the Gospel: people hear about Jesus and come to him (for example, 1:45; 5:27; 10:47). However, the disciples definitely oppose it and rebuke those bringing the children. Mark heightens the power of Jesus' statement by noting his indignation and adding the Master's direct *command* that the children be brought to him.

There have been countless interpretations of what being "like a child" means. Mark does not tell us. I have found the observations of Dan Via[11] especially helpful. Using Carl Jung's archetype of the child, Via shows how it fits into Mark's perspective and argument: children are essentially in transit and change. They must take risks and abandon security in order to become truly independent. Adults tend to become hardened and settled in their ways. Jesus challenges adults to become children again and thus open to change and renewal. This means risk and the willingness that the Gospel speaks of to "lose one's life." Dan Via writes,

> The adult has become hardened in heart, so that the inner center of life is not open to a different future. Thus if one is to have life, one must make the move that one had not made before. One must move back to childhood and begin again. This en-

tails renouncing the shape of one's present existence in order
to recover an abandoned potential. Life must be lost in order
to be found. The very terminology of the loss of life expresses
the radicalness of this move.[12]

Thus, as Via notes, the decision to become a child is the
key to participation in the central death/resurrection theme of
Mark. Making one's self a child is a way to pass through death
and overcome its powers. Various Gospel characters illustrate
this change by taking on themselves a new story as they follow Jesus even to Jerusalem and the cross. An example is the
blind Bartimaeus who receives his sight and follows Jesus along
the way (10:46-52).

The transitional image of the child sheds light on other
teachings of Jesus about facing the difficult realities of life by
deciding to make a new beginning, framed between the two
children's stories, we find the teaching of Jesus on marriage
and divorce. Jesus appeals to his audience to start anew from
the beginning of God's creation to find a model for the
covenant between man and woman (10:6). Then, after the children's blessing, the story of the encounter of Jesus with the
rich man stresses the need to start life afresh and break away
from the patterns of adult life that are often based on the security of material possessions. Jesus tells the rich man, "You
lack one thing; go, sell what you have, and give to the poor,
and you will have treasure in heaven; and come, follow me"
(10:21).

## The Mysterious Youngster Who Follows Jesus After His Arrest

Mark tells us that all of Jesus' male disciples fled at his arrest and abandoned him (14:50). While this is shocking, it is
certainly understandable for they might very well have en-
dured a horrible crucifixion along with Jesus. However, only
the Gospel of Mark records the following story of a brave

youngster who continued to follow Jesus at great risk even after the Master had been arrested: "A young man followed him, with nothing but a linen cloth about his body; and they seized him, but he left the linen cloth and ran away naked" (14:51-52).

This story about the youth is important for us as a climax to Jesus' teaching about the primacy of the children and the young in his kingdom. It is only this youngster (along with the women at the foot of the cross) who dares to follow Jesus at the risk of his own life during the dark hour of Jesus' arrest. Mark teaches his audience that God turns the tables on human expectations by working through the "weakness" of little ones rather than through the "strength" of the world's older and more powerful people. The mystery of the Cross reverses all human expectations.

However, there is a sequel to this mysterious story. When Mary Magdalene and the other women came to the tomb on Easter morning at sunrise, they said to one another, "Who will roll away the stone for us from the door of the tomb?" (16:3). Then the text notes, "Entering the tomb, they saw a young man sitting on the right side, dressed in a white robe; and they were amazed" (16:5). There are notable similarities[13] between this story and the story of the young man at the arrest of Jesus: the same Greek word for "young man," *neaniskos*, is used. Also the same word, "clothed" is found in the two stories. There seems to be a contrast[14] between the garb in the second story and the previous state of the young man who fled naked after losing his only clothing, a linen cloth, and ran away naked, thus facing shame and disgrace. Now, instead, he has a white robe of triumph and victory. This "white robe" is also used in the Book of Revelation to describe those who have faced suffering or martyrdom for their faith (6:11; 7:9, 13, 14).

The central place of the young man in Mark's resurrection story may be discovered by close attention to the text: "Very early when the sun had risen, on the first day of the week, they came to the tomb. They were saying to one another, 'who will roll back the stone for us from the entrance to the tomb?' '' (16:3). The Greek imperfect verb form, ''they were saying,'' emphasizes the women's continued concern on their way to the tomb. It was essential for them to actually enter the tomb to carry out their intended anointing (16:1). Their question hints that this moving of the stone would be physically impossible for them without considerable outside help.

''When they looked up, they saw that the stone had been rolled back; it was very great'' (16:4). The women continue to focus their attention on the stone as they arrive, look up, and *notice* that the stone has already been rolled back. The author then justifies the women's concern by observing that ''the stone was very great'' (16:4). The natural sequence after the preoccupation about the stone's removal and the comment about its size suggests that they are amazed to conclude that the young man sitting inside is the only possible agent of such a prodigious feat.

Since this suggestion is new[15] and sheds new light on the centrality of the youth in the climax of Mark's Gospel, it is important to substantiate it carefully by the following considerations.

*1. In objection, it might be claimed that the women are amazed at the appearance of the young man because they regard him as an angel.* After all, Matthew makes this identification and has an angel of God roll back the stone in 28:2. In response, Mark refers explicitly to angels in other texts when he wishes to do so (1:13; 8:38; 12:25; 13:27, 32). For this reason among others, A. K. Jenkins[16] has argued that it is very unlikely that *neaniskos*, ''young man or youth'' could refer to an angel. Again, it could be argued that the women were amazed to see the empty tomb. On the other hand, in the text the women's attention has been directed first to the stone and then to the youngster seated by the tomb. As yet, there has been no mention about Jesus' body not being there. This only comes later with the young man's announcement and commission to the women.

*2. All of Mark's Gospel leads to the resurrection proclamation and commission in 16:7.* It would be extremely important for the Gospel writer to support the young man's announcement by an unmistakable sign from God. Mark has already taken care to provide remarkable signs to support central sayings/actions of Jesus. For example, the mysterious finding of the donkey when the disciples follow Jesus' directions prepares the way for his entry into Jerusalem (11:1-7); the sign of the fig tree (11:12-14, 20-21) is a miracle and literary frame supporting Jesus' authoritative words/actions concerning the Temple and its new meaning (11:15-18). The power of Jesus' word demonstrated by its effect on the fig tree shows that his word about the Temple is just as sure and effective. Jesus' directions to his disciples to enter the city and follow a man carrying a jug of water to a prepared guest room seem to be a sign of the extraordinary importance of the Last Supper (14:12-16).

Such actions follow the biblical pattern of looking for a divine sign to support words or events that will have great meaning (Isa 7:10; Gen 24:12-14). It would be unusual if no sign or confirmation supported the final Gospel proclamation made by a mere youth. Other sources preserve the extraordinary nature of the rolled stone at the tomb. Matthew has an earthquake and an angel of God moving the stone. Matthew changes Mark's young man into an angel who becomes part of a light-filled theophany to further enhance the resurrection proclamation (28:2-7). The Gospel of Peter, chapter 9, has the stone mysteriously roll away by itself.

*3. The remarkable biblical parallel to the rolled stone at Jesus' tomb.* We must beware of "parallelomania" or making conclusions because of similarities. Yet it must be remembered that what we often call coincidences were not such for Mark and his audience who considered them part of a divine plan. For the author, it was no coincidence that the soldiers divided Jesus' garments among them by lot, but part of a mysterious divine plan in accord with the Scriptures of Psalm 22:18 (Mark 15:24). The same could be said of Jesus' statements about the fig tree and of his preparations for the entry into Jerusalem and the Last Supper. With their knowledge of the Scriptures, Mark and his audience would certainly be aware of a remarkable miracle in Genesis that made possible the beginnings of the people of Israel. By himself, their father Jacob rolled the large stone from the well in Paddan-Aram to water the flocks of his cousin Rachel. We need to see the text in order to point out the unusual convergences:

> As he [Jacob] looked, he saw a well in the field, and lo, three flocks of sheep lying beside it; for out of that well the flocks were watered. *The stone* on the well's mouth *was large,* and when all the flocks were gathered there, the shepherds would *roll the stone* from the mouth of the well, and water the sheep, and put the *stone* back in its place upon the mouth of the well (Gen 29:2-3).

Jacob then greets the shepherds, who inform him that Rachel is coming to the well with her flocks. Because the stone is too heavy, the shepherds explain that they cannot water the flocks until all the shepherds are gathered together and *the stone is rolled* from the mouth of the well (Gen 29:8). When Jacob saw Rachel approach the well, he went up, and *rolled the stone* (Gen 29:10) from the well's mouth and watered the flock of Laban, his mother's brother. Jacob's remarkable feat was significant because it was undeniable evidence of God's presence with him which he had just been promised in a dream at Bethel (Gen 28:10-22). With this impressive "miracle" as a sign from God, Laban accepts Jacob into his family and gives him his own daughters in marriage. This is a formative biblical marriage; from it will come the birth of the people of Israel.

The textual details in the Greek version (LXX) of the Old Testament merit special notice. The *rolling of the stone* is mentioned three times (Gen 29:3, 8, 10) corresponding to the triple use in Mark 15:46; 16:3, 4. The Greek verb "roll," *apokyliō*, used in the LXX is the same as that in Mark 16:3, 4. This verb is found only twice in the Old Testament, once here in connection with the well stone and elsewhere only in another context in Judith 13:9 when she rolled Holofornes' beheaded body off the bed. The description of the stone in the LXX and Mark is nearly identical: "The stone was great," *lithos de ēn megas* (Gen 29:2) and *ho lithos ēn gar megas* (Mark 16:4).

In addition, the atmosphere for the miracle in Mark and in Genesis is similar. The purpose of Jacob's miracle is that he, as a shepherd, will be able to water the flocks of Rachel and her family. This result is mentioned again and again (Gen 29:2, 3, 8, 10). It is a prelude to a great announcement when Rachel runs to tell Laban what has happened (Gen 29:12). By means of the miracle, Jacob literally becomes the shepherd and leader of Israel. The purpose of Mark's miracle is similar and has the same pastoral context. Jesus had predicted that the shepherd would be struck and the sheep scattered without nourishment but that he would rise and go before his sheep once more (14:27-28). At the tomb, the miraculous rolling away of the stone certifies the great announcement that follows: Jesus, the shepherd, will once again gather his sheep together in Galilee and nourish them as before (16:7). Like Rachel running to tell her family, the women in Mark hear the announcement and run from the tomb (16:8).

4. *The young man and the symbolism of the rolled away stone.* The symbolism of the action of both the young man and Jacob strengthens our thesis. In regard to Jacob, Robert Alter has noted the following, "The well at an oasis is obviously a symbol of fertility and, in all likelihood, also a female symbol."[17] The purpose of Jacob's journey is to obtain a wife and chil-

dren. However, "he has an obstacle to overcome—the stone on the mouth of the well."[18] Jerome Neyrey[19] has also drawn attention to the symbolic meaning of Jacob's well in its connection with spirit, new life, and cleansing. The Genesis text itself focuses on the goal of Jacob's action which is the watering of the sheep of his new house and family that he is about to undertake as shepherd (Gen 29:3, 7, 8, 10).

The symbolism of the rolling away of the stone from Jesus' tomb signifying a victory over death and its power is not a new idea. There are, for example, the more recent studies of Robert Couffignal[20] and Eugene Laverdiere.[21] But with an understanding of the young man's role, the symbolism is much more easily identified in Mark's dramatic narrative. First, the author emphasizes the definitiveness of Jesus' death. Pilate himself verifies it by summoning the centurion who had supervised Jesus' execution and witnessed his death (15:44-45). Then Joseph of Arimathea, a respectable witness, takes the body down from the cross, wraps it in burial clothes, and places it in the tomb. As a final seal and sign of the power of death, he rolls a stone *against* the tomb entrance (15:46). The special verb *proskyliō*, "to roll against," emphasizes the final closure, the stone seal of death which no one can possibly remove.

On the other hand, the opening of a tomb can signify an encounter with all the powers of death and a victory over them. In Mark's Gospel, the youth's action in rolling away the stone may symbolize a victory over the powers of death. Humanly speaking, no one has the power to "roll away the stone" and conquer death. Yet Mark's view of the ideal disciple provides a way. God gives to those like the anonymous youth who risk their life to follow Jesus the power to roll it away, partake of the power of the resurrection, and announce it to the world.

*excellent*

5. *Mark's foreshadowing of the tomb story.* If the action of the youthful disciple is so central to Mark's climax, we would expect some foreshadowing of it in accord with dramatic tech-

niques. In 5:1-20, the author devotes unusual attention to the powerful exorcism of the man in Gerasa (some texts). This has a Gentile flavor with the description of the two thousand pigs that rush off the cliff and drown in the sea after the demons enter them. The scene has details which suggest all the symbolism of death and the powers of evil. Here, also, we have a man of prodigious strength (and no clothes) whom no one is able to bind even with chains. He is possessed by hordes of evil spirits. His dwelling place is in cemeteries and tombs (5:2, 3). Yet Jesus by his power frees him from the powers of the evil spirits and death (his dwelling among the tombs). The man who was possessed becomes tame, puts on his clothes once more, and sits by Jesus. He desires to go with Jesus, but instead Jesus tells him "go home to your friends, and tell them how much the Lord has done for you, and how he has had mercy on you" (5:20, RSV). He obeys Jesus and becomes the first follower to proclaim his deeds in the Gentile atmosphere of the cities of the Decapolis (5:20).

The symbolic identification/contrast of the man at Gerasa to the young man at Jesus' tomb is not hard to find. Both men are associated with the tomb: one with the totality of the powers of death, the other with removing the stone and thus obtaining victory over death. Both of them are strong: one with the powers of death and evil spirits which no one can overcome, the other with the limitless power of God which alone can open up the tombs of death. The first man sits down at Jesus' side; the second sits by the tomb as a teacher. The first man desires to be *with* Jesus; the second actually fulfills this desire by following *with* him as far as his arrest. The former demoniac is the first to proclaim Jesus' word at his actual command, "Go, tell your friends and those in your house" (5:19). Paralleling this, the youth at the tomb becomes the chosen herald of Jesus' resurrection to others: "Go, tell his disciples and Peter that he is going before you to Galilee" (16:5).

There may be other foreshadowing or symbolic features not easily contrasted: premature age and death associated with the man among the tombs in the fifth chapter of Mark in contrast with the literally rejuvenated *youth, neaniskos,* at Jesus' tomb. There may be some connection between the inability to *bind* the strong man in Mark 5:3-4 and the attempted arrest of the young man in Mark 14:52, since Mark connects binding with arrest (6:17; 15:1, 7). The parallel mention of stones is intriguing. The demoniac had been "bruising himself with stones" (5:5). This need not mean self-inflicted injuries, but rather bruising himself *on* the large stones that he had to move in order to live within the tombs. This hints at a certain ability to move them that could prepare the way for the rolling of the stone in 16:4.

## The Young Man in the Dramatic Climax of Mark's Gospel

In view of what we have observed about the young man and the rolled stone, we can discover a new special place for the young man in Mark's dramatic sequence. This will prove true if the young man appears as a surprising counterpart of Jesus, the hero of the whole drama. Our attention must go back to the young man, *neaniskos,* found only in Mark 14:51: "Now a young man followed him wearing nothing but a linen cloth about his body. They seized him, but he left the cloth behind and ran off naked." The young man appears quite distinct and even in opposition to the previous fleeing disciples in 14:50; the seizing of Jesus is especially highlighted by the repetition of the verb *krateō,* "seize" (14:1, 44, 46, 49). The other disciples fled and were unwilling to face seizure or arrest. However, the young man continued to follow Jesus even after he had been *seized* once already leaving himself open to be *seized* (14:51) again and thus imitate Jesus. In being stripped of his garments, he also becomes like Jesus stripped of his garments by the soldiers at the cross (15:24). Of course—like the other disciples—the young man did flee, but this was to escape *after* he was arrested. At least it could be said that he was one step ahead of the other disciples.

This leaves the way open for seeing our youth as the model for the Gospel audience. Discipleship meaning to follow Jesus in suffering is a dominant theme in Mark. In describing the young man as a disciple, Mark uses the stronger form of the verb "to follow," *synakoloutheō;* he uses it elsewhere only in 5:37 to refer to Peter, James, and John who are permitted to witness the raising of Jairus' daughter. In Jesus' last testament, Mark has emphasized that those who are arrested and delivered up to councils, synagogues, kings, and governors will give testimony, *martyrion* (13:9), and as a result the Gospel will be preached to the world as the necessary prelude to Jesus' return (13:10). The anonymous young man is the first follower to be actually arrested and merits to be first to actually know of the resurrection by entering the tomb through a great feat of miraculous strength. He is also the first to proclaim the resurrection to others.

The fact that he escaped his arresters and fled away naked does not detract from his willingness to risk arrest and death by following Jesus. The white-robe-of-victory clothing contrasts a previous state in which the same young man was disrobed and shamed before others when he fled naked as a consequence of his decision to face arrest like Jesus.

The mysterious youth in Mark risks his life by following Jesus even after the other disciples had fled. Thus he participates in Jesus' victory over death. He opens the sealed tomb by a prodigious feat of strength and sits beside it in the attitude of a teacher for the Gospel audience. In this way, the Gospel ends in a great surprise: God works in a very special manner through a mere youth, not through the chosen inner circle of the Twelve nor through Jesus' close women associates. In addition, if the foreshadowing in 5:1-20 is correct, the authority (or author) behind the Gospel may be an anonymous young disciple from the Decapolis region (5:20) where only this Gospel reports a miracle performed by Jesus (7:31). This man sat by Jesus, wanted to remain with him, but Jesus sent him out as his first apostle (even before the mission of the Twelve in 6:7) to tell the news of his conversion to his own people in the Decapolis (5:20).

There is also another symbolism connected with the image of the child within all of us who needs to emerge and be renewed. Mark intends to connect the message of Jesus' resurrection to new life and rejuvenation. The way to renewed youth is to forget one's self as this mysterious disciple did and follow Jesus, even at great risk. This attitude breaks through the sealed stone barriers of death and time and opens the way to participate in Jesus' resurrection even during one's own lifetime.

With the resurrection proclamation, Mark's Gospel ends with a double surprise. The Gospel had begun with Jesus' first words to his disciples in Galilee, "Follow me and I will make you fishers of human beings" (1:17). Yet the male disciples all abandon Jesus at his arrest. Only Mary Magdalene and the other women follow him all the way from Galilee to the cross and make the fishing apostolate of the Twelve a reality by bringing the news to Peter and the others of Jesus' resurrection. The second surprise is the youngster who had the courage to continue to follow Jesus after his arrest and then went to the tomb on Easter morning where he rolled aside the tomb stone with miraculous strength and became the first to discover the empty tomb and announce the mystery of the resurrection to others.

**In Conclusion**

Mark's audience lived in a tense atmosphere caused by Roman persecution and abusive power. The Roman War with the Jews was a signal to some prophets and teachers that Jesus would soon return with temporal power to help Christians overcome their persecutors. In contrast, Mark proclaims that true liberation can only come by imitation of Jesus' own way of the cross. This means that Christ's followers must be willing to suffer or even die for what they believe in. Only by putting their lives on the line can they witness to the Romans the truth of what they believe in. In doing this, they imitate Jesus who even won over his executioner, the Roman centurion, by the way that he suffered and died. This faithful witness of Mark's audience will eventually win over their Roman persecutors and bring about the awaited return of Jesus.

Jesus is the hero of the Gospel by the way that he voluntarily accepts arrest, trial, and sufferings. The counterparts of Jesus are those who follow him as far as the cross. To our surprise, they turn out to be women and children, not the male disciples who all fled at his arrest. Mary Magdalene and the other women are the only ones to follow Jesus from Galilee all the way to the cross.

Jesus promises that the children, who are at the lowest rung of society's ladder, will be his true successors. He does this through the children's stories within the three central discipleship sections in Mark's Gospel. Jesus' blessing of children has central significance in view of the meaning of the biblical ritual blessings used by Isaac, Jacob, and Joseph to designate and empower their successors. The illustrations in Mark also point out that children will not only have priority in the kingdom but will provide living examples of what the kingdom is all about.

The example of the youngster who fled naked at Jesus' arrest provides a surprising climax to Mark's Gospel. The descriptions of the young man at Jesus' tomb are very similar. Moreover, the miracle of the rolling of the stone can be attributed to him if we bear in mind the important rolling-stone miracle which enabled Jacob to recognize his cousin Rachel at the well and to eventually fulfill God's plan of numerous descendants for him. If this all goes together, the resurrection proclamation of the young man brings to a climax Mark's theme that children and the young have priority in the kingdom. They are the first to be liberated by Jesus and the ones who play the decisive role in liberating others. True liberation from Roman oppression as well as from the abuse of power by Christian leaders can only come about through granting a first place to children.

## 2

# The Priority of Little Ones: Matthew's Gospel

## The Situation of Matthew's Community[22]

What Mark's Gospel has taught about children cannot simply be transferred to Matthew. This Gospel was written for another audience living in an entirely new situation. For our purposes, we will outline some significant differences affecting Matthew's treatment of children.

In Mark, we noted that his community, of non-Jewish Christians faced the severe crisis of heavy persecution under abusive Roman authority. The community felt that Jesus would return soon and that the best way they could hasten his coming was by preaching the Gospel through the personal example of their lives. If they patiently suffered and even died for their faith as Jesus had done, they could win over their Roman oppressors just as Jesus had won over his own executioner, the Roman centurion. However, in Matthew, this is not a primary concern. The Gospel references to Gentile persecution are much fewer in number; instead, there are more descriptions of friction between Jewish-Christians and their own countrymen. So there is no longer a priority given to hastening Jesus' return by preaching the Gospel to the world through the witness of martyrdom. There must be another means to do this: hearing and keeping Jesus' word while being identified with him.

The quality of time in Matthew also enhances the authoritative words of Jesus. No longer, as in Mark, do many believers feel that there will be a relatively short time before Jesus' return. Instead, some Gospel stories suggest a longer period of waiting and a community attitude of looking toward an extended history in this world. In the parable of the householder, the steward begins to mistreat slaves under him because he says to himself, "My master is delayed" (24:48). In the parable of the talents, the master returns to settle his accounts "after a long time" (25:19). In the parable of the ten virgins, the bridesmaids fall asleep because the "bridegroom was delayed" (25:5). In each of these stories, Jesus warns the Gospel audience to be vigilant and attentive to good works. The Master will surely return, but the time is uncertain and most people will be caught unaware in the midst of ordinary daily activities.

Another decisive factor in Matthew's message is the situation of the community in relation to Judaism. Most of the Gospel audience seem to be Jewish Christians still carefully observing the Mosaic biblical laws and customs. Unlike Mark, Matthew has no need to explain them to his audience. However, there is much tension in the Gospel between Jewish Christians and their Jewish brothers and sisters. An important divisive event was the war with Rome where Christians were branded as traitors because they would not fight against Rome under the leadership of military leaders who posed as Messiahs. Jesus had warned them not to fight but to flee to the mountains (24:15-18).

After the war with Rome, there was further tension between Jewish Christians and their fellow Jews because the Pharisees strengthened their leadership over the people. This meant that the Pharisaic brand of Judaism became more and more the religion of the people. Consequently, they tended to suspect Jewish Christians and regard them as "heretics." The Gospel mentions insults and ostracism from the synagogue as the experience of some Christians (10:17; 5:11).

The destruction of Jerusalem and the Temple was also a time of crisis for Jewish Christians. They had always looked to Jerusalem as their religious capital, their center of authority. The Bible taught that there was a succession of legitimate religious authority from God to Moses to the teachers of Israel. Where could they turn now for authoritative teachings? The Pharisees had previously been their revered teachers to whom they looked for assurance, authority, and answers. With the loss of Jerusalem as their religious capital, some Christians were tempted to return to their former teachers or become only secret Christians.

Another disturbing element for Jewish Christians was the growing majority of Gentile converts in many churches. Jewish Christians, faithful to their traditional Jewish customs, were finding it more and more difficult to feel at home with Gentile community members who did not show the same respect for biblical laws and customs not part of their culture that would be strange to their family and friends. As a result, some Jewish Christians were tempted to return to Judaism; others chose to leave and establish their own communities across the Jordan where they could strictly practice all their biblical and traditional observances, believe in Jesus as the Christ, but not live side by side with Gentiles.

To respond to the needs of his audience, Matthew has to present a strong image of Jesus as an authoritative teacher who has appointed others to succeed him. He has entrusted his teachings to them, and his words that they echo carry his own authority and presence. The former sequence of Jewish teaching was God-Moses-Jewish teachers (especially the Pharisees), people. Now it will be God-Jesus (as a new Moses), the Twelve, especially Peter, and the people. The first chapters of the Gospel introduce Jesus as a new Moses and authoritative Messiah. Beginning with the geneology, they recount as proof the extraordinary events of his birth and childhood. The great discourses of the Gospel, especially the Sermon on the Mount, establish the authority of Jesus' words and teachings as superior to those given by God to Moses on Mount Sinai and as ways of higher perfection than the teachings of the scribes and Pharisees.

The third part of the succession of legitimate teachers is found particularly in the special material about Peter and the authority of the *ekklēsia* of which he will be the rock and foundation. He and his successors will hold the keys of the kingdom and the power of authorized teachers (16:13-20). I say "successors" because Peter was almost certainly dead by the time Matthew's Gospel was written around the end of the first century, so the words seem to refer to a teacher or teachers who hold his authority.

The final or fourth part of the succession comes at the final mountain scene or "graduation ceremony" when the new teachers are empowered to bring Jesus' teachings to the world, assured that Jesus' presence and power will be with them as they faithfully transmit his instructions. In the story of Jesus' death, Matthew emphasizes the power and authority of Jesus as son of God in order to prepare for this final scene. There is an earthquake at the moment of his death and when the women come to visit his tomb. The earthquake causes the mountain to split and tombs to open; bodies of the just arise and appear to many. These extraordinary events are part of a tremendous explosion of power caused by Jesus' death and resurrection. The centurion and those with him are amazed and exclaim, "Truly this was the son of God" (27:54).

The last mountain scene is like an enthronement ritual as Jesus appears to the Eleven, gives them his own power, and sends them out into the world while assuring them of his continual presence. The final words of the Gospel are:

> All authority in heaven and on earth has been given to me. Go therefore and make disciples of all nations, baptizing them in

the name of the Father and of the Son and of the Holy Spirit, teaching them to observe all that I have commanded you; and lo, I am with you always, to the close of the age (28:18-20).

## Jesus as the Chosen Child and Model for Matthew's Audience

Matthew's interest in children begins in the first pages of his Gospel with his emphasis on Jesus as *The Child*. This is so because he has in mind the scriptural prophecies about the coming great Child and descendant of David that we considered in Part I. The story of Jesus' birth and childhood also is a fitting introduction to the rest of the Gospel where the priority of children and little ones will be a central theme. Jesus as a child becomes a model for the Christian as a child.

Matthew begins his Gospel by showing his audience that God has been working in the births of children for thousands of years to prepare the way for the birth of the child Jesus. Among these births, there are some extraordinary ones. The first, to Abraham and Sarah, is a birth so humanly impossible that both parents laughed when they heard about it. So they called their son Isaac, which means "laughter." Then, a hated foreigner, a Moabite, becomes the great-great grandfather of King David, through Ruth. Such was the disdain for Moabites that no Moabite, even to the tenth generation, could take part in the assembly of Israel (Deut 23:3). God's work in the birth of children and new life is not even impeded by the fact that David became father of King Solomon as the result of adultery followed by murder (1:6). All these births prepare the way for the most remarkable birth of all: "Now the birth of Jesus Christ took place in this way" (1:18).

This last child is the most unlikely, from a human point of view, to be the long awaited one to fulfill the prophecies. Joseph somehow discovered that Mary, his future spouse, had become pregnant. Knowing the child was not his, he immediately made plans for a private divorce (1:19). He knew very well the biblical laws stating that a bastard child and its descendants were so disgraced that no offspring, even to the tenth generation, could ever take a place in the community of Israel (Deut 23:2). Yet an angel informs him in a dream that the unexpected child is of the Holy Spirit and that he should not hesitate to go on with the marriage (1:20). The angel tells him to call the boy Jesus. Ironically, a child considered to be born in sin is the one who will save others from sin according to the meaning of his name. Matthew thus prepares for a central Gospel theme that the last and the least, as exemplified by children, will be the first in God's kingdom.

Matthew goes on to state that Mary, the "unwed mother," fulfills in a mysterious way the prophecy of Isaiah that a great future child will be born to the dynasty of David: "All this took place to fulfill what the Lord had spoken by the prophet: 'Behold a virgin shall conceive and bear a son, and his name shall be called Emmanuel [which means, God with us]'" (1:23). The extraordinary name informs the Gospel audience that God is indeed present in this unusual child. He is presented as the example for all future children and Christians since the Gospel will end on a similar note: Jesus tells his disciples in his final words on the Galilee mountain, "I am with you always, to the close of the age" (28:20). First, God will be Emmanuel through the birth of the child Jesus. Then he will be Emmanuel in every Christian through the presence of Jesus.

It is surprising that the word and sign of Emmanuel has almost been forgotten by believers. Every year, I ask my college and graduate students what "Noel" means, a word familiar to everyone in Christmas songs and on greeting cards. I have yet to receive a correct answer. It is actually an old French abbreviation of "Emmanuel." Perhaps the word "Noel" became so commonplace around Christmas that its original meaning became lost!

*Noel = Emmanuel*

After the opening genealogy, Matthew describes the unusual events that took place at the time this child was born. In doing so, Matthew is also summarizing the whole meaning of Jesus' life. The evangelist tells how The Child is sought by the wise men of the East who see his star and come to worship him (2:2). However, the newly born "king of the Jews" is opposed by the Jewish King Herod who fears him as a rival (2:2-3). The chief priests and scribes tell Herod about the remarkable child who will be born at Bethlehem, according to the Scriptures. The king sends the wise men there to search for *the child*, asking the Magi to bring word back to him so that he might also come and worship him.

In chapter two, Matthew uses the expression, "the child" nine times, no doubt because he wants his audience to keep in mind *the child* God promised the prophet Isaiah. This series begins with Herod's direction to the wise men, "Go and search diligently for *the child*, and when you have found him bring me word, that I too may come and worship him" (2:9). It continues with the description of the finding of the child: "The star which they had seen in the East went before them, till it came to rest over the place where *the child* was. . . . Going into the house they saw *the child* with Mary his mother, and they fell down and worshiped him" (2:9-10). Thus the first part of the series ends with worshiping *the child* and then offering him gifts of gold, frankincense, and myrrh.

The next five statements describe the atmosphere of suffering in the childhood events. An angel of the Lord appeared to Joseph in a dream and said, "Rise, take *the child* and his mother, and flee to Egypt, and remain there till I tell you; for Herod is about to search for *the child* to destroy him." Joseph immediately obeyed the divine command: "He rose and took *the child* and his mother by night, and departed to Egypt, and remained there until the death of Herod" (2:13-15).

These descriptions of a persecuted child also fit those of the

wonderful child described in Isaiah the prophet. That child was
to grow up in a land devastated by war and terror. God had
told Isaiah that before the child knew how "to refuse the evil
and choose the good his country would suffer one of the
greatest disasters of its history" (Isaiah 7:16-17). The descriptions of the child's flight into Egypt focus on the same theme.
Egypt was traditionally as well as symbolically the land of slav-
ery and oppression. In going to Egypt, *the child* became one
with all the sufferings and hardships undergone by his people
throughout history and identified with them.

The child, then, really represents all his people. He grows
up in an atmosphere of terrible violence. Herod, realizing the
Magi have tricked him, orders all the male children in the
region of Bethlehem who are two years and under to be put
to death (2:16). Matthew, with his concern for Scripture, pictures Rachel, the mother of the family of Israel, weeping for
her children (2:18). Matthew will later bring this identification
theme into his Gospel by showing how Jesus identifies with
children and the least in the kingdom.

Matthew's *child* is not only the wondrous child in Isaiah
but also similar to Moses, the great liberator who freed Israel
from Egypt. We saw earlier that the parallel to Moses was important for Matthew's Gospel. Moses' life was threatened as
a child by the Pharaoh's decree that all newly born infants were
to be put to death (Exod 1:15-16). However, Moses' mother
saved her child by hiding him, and Pharaoh's daughter found
him floating on the Nile river in a basket (Exod 2:1-10). Later,
when the young Moses fought and killed an Egyptian while
defending a fellow Hebrew, Pharaoh tried to kill him. As a
result, he was forced to leave Egypt (Exod 2:11-15). In the Sinai
Peninsula, God appeared to Moses and told him to return to
Egypt to liberate his people. God said to him, "Go back to
Egypt; for the men who were seeking your life are dead" (Exod
4:19). This seems to be a deliberate parallel to the angel of the

Lord appearing in a dream to Joseph and saying, ''Rise, take the child and his mother and go to the land of Israel, for those who sought the child's life are dead'' (Matt 2:20).

We can now sum up the purpose behind Matthew's first two chapters on the birth and childhood of Jesus. He is first of all concerned to show the fulfillment of Scriptures, which for him are the divine plan. Jesus' virgin birth indicates he is the promised child prophesied by Isaiah. God reverses and confounds human expectations by choosing a child to save his people. In this child who is the Emmanuel, God is with his people, all of God's power will be at work. The child will also be the hope of the world, as illustrated by the Magi whose journey is guided by God through a star and by dreams.

This child is also one with this people in their suffering, especially their exile in Egypt. Herod, the Jewish king, tries to kill the ''newly born king,'' afraid that he himself might be supplanted by him. The experience of the child Jesus is also a remarkable parallel to that of Moses. Moses liberated his people at the risk of his life, just as the child suffered exile and danger to his life in order to be a true liberator of his people.

The story of Jesus' childhood in Matthew is really a summary of the whole Gospel message. Jesus will be rejected by the leaders of his country, but this will open up the way for the Gentiles (the Magi from the East) to follow the star of faith and come to him in worship. The importance that Matthew attaches to Jesus' childhood is especially important for us, since it prepares the way for a central Gospel teaching on the priority of little ones as models of discipleship.

### The Last and Least and Little Ones in Matthew

When studying Mark, we found his first story about children in a central location after Jesus' second prediction of his suffering and death. The mention of death would suggest to the Gospel audience succession to Jesus. Consequently, it was quite significant to them that the Twelve had been arguing as they went along about which of them would be the greatest in the coming kingdom. To make a public lesson, Jesus brought forward a child and stood him in their midst, suggesting that his true successors will be children. Immediately we notice great differences in Matthew. There is no contrast to the Twelve at all. In fact, Matthew inserts here a story about Peter that would enhance his authority. This story is about the obligation of the Temple tax and Jesus' mysterious order to Peter to go fishing, open the mouth of a fish, and pay the temple tax with the money he finds there. Then Matthew opens up a whole new section of Jesus' teachings beginning with a central emphasis on children in the community:

> At that time the disciples came to Jesus, saying, "Who is the greatest in the kingdom of heaven?" And calling to him a child, he put him in the midst of them, and said, "Truly, I say to you, unless you turn and become like children, you will never enter the kingdom of heaven. Whoever humbles himself like this child, he is the greatest in the kingdom of heaven. Whoever receives one such child in my name receives me; but whoever causes one of these little ones who believe in me to sin, it would be better for him to have a great millstone fastened around his neck and to be drowned in the depth of the sea (18:1-6).

Instead of the sharp contrast to the Twelve in Mark's Gospel, we find here a simple question addressed to Jesus concerning the matter of priority and importance in the kingdom. Children are addressed, first of all, because they are the prototype for all the "little ones," as well as the "last and least" in Matthew's Gospel. This is especially true of the examples that will be given in chapter 18. This chapter stands apart as a central discourse in Matthew with its closing literary formula, "When Jesus had finished these sayings. . . ." (19:1). Actually, Matthew's approach will heighten the importance of children for they will stand for a much larger group and introduce a key section of teachings in this Gospel. Matthew's treatment of children will in some ways be more revolutionary than Mark's for children stand for the last and least in the kingdom and are the models for all disciples of Jesus.

The image of a child will have an important variety of meanings in Matthew: first of all, the introduction, "Unless you turn and become like children, you will never enter the kingdom of heaven" (18:3). The word "turn" in biblical usage often means conversion and repentance. Returning to childhood would mean starting life all over again with new relationships and fresh experiences. Thus, a child is an image of the newness of Christian life. Every believer must begin life all over again in complete renewal in order to be Jesus' disciple.

A second image is found in the next saying of Jesus, "Whoever humbles himself like this child is the greatest in the kingdom of heaven" (18:1-3). This humbling of oneself is not an exterior quality but an inner one. Jesus describes himself as "meek and humble of heart" (11:29) because he does not impose himself on people and put heavy burdens on them: "My yoke is easy and my burden is light" (11:30). Soon afterward he likens himself to the humble servant of the Lord in the prophet Isaiah, who does not "wrangle or cry aloud, nor will any one hear his voice in the streets; he will not break a bruised reed or quench a smoldering wick till he brings justice to victory" (12:19-20; Isaiah 42:1-4).

Children may be examples of humility because they do not force themselves on others or rely on aggressive tactics. Later, Matthew records Jesus' saying, "Whoever exalts himself will be humbled, and whoever humbles himself will be exalted" (23:12). Matthew likes to emphasize this theme as God's way of reversing human values. Jesus says, "Many that are first will be last, and the last first." Also, "The last will be first, and the first last" (19:30; 20:16). Once again, children fit this image very well.

The next saying is, "Whoever receives one such child in my name receives me." In Mark's context, we suggested that succession to Jesus was reflected in these words. However, in Matthew, there is no contrast to the disciples. It is more likely that these words fit in with the theme of identification with Jesus that is so strong in this gospel, something we will later expand upon. The contrast is "whoever causes one of these little ones to sin" is guilty of a sin deserving a most severe punishment (18:6). Here Matthew expands the concept from children to "little ones," giving a much broader scope to his image of the child.

Next, the importance of the "little ones" is stressed by Jesus' declaration that each "little one" has a special guardian angel assigned by God to look after him or her: "See that you do not despise one of these little ones; for I tell you that in heaven their angels always behold the face of my Father who is in heaven" (18:10). This doctrine of guardian angels is first found in later Judaism: the angel Raphael in the Book of Tobit is an example.

In Matthew, this concern for each "little one" in particular is emphasized in the parable of the lost sheep where the "little one" also becomes a single lost member of the community:

> What do you think? If a man has a hundred sheep, and one of them has gone astray, does he not leave the ninety-nine on the mountains and go in search of the one that went astray? And if he finds it, truly, I say to you, he rejoices over it more than over the ninety-nine that never went astray (18:12-13).

This parable is a striking example of the priority of the little ones: first, the anxious search for the one lost, even if it means leaving the other ninety-nine temporarily. Then, the joy in finding the lost sheep tells the community that their greatest moments of happiness will result from such care of little ones. The ending of the parable is sealed by a summary statement to emphasize its importance and to make it clear that commu-

*[handwritten margin note: Biblical reference to Guardian Angel]*

*[handwritten note at bottom: X So, if you 'change and become like a little child,' you merit a special Guardian Angel]*

nity concern for little ones is nothing less than God's own care in action: "So it is not the will of my Father who is in heaven that one of these little ones should perish" (18:14).

Matthew adds two more examples of this search for the lost and "little ones." The first is the case of a serious transgression within the community. The approach to the sinner is to be gentle and gradual: first privately, one to one; then if that fails, with two or three witnesses; finally as a last resort, an appeal to the whole community to bring the transgressor to his or her senses. Only when all else fails will the community temporarily exclude the lost one (18:15).

Peter's question introduces a final example: "Lord, how often shall my brother sin against me, and I forgive him? As many as seven times?" Jesus answers, "I do not say to you seven times but seventy times seven" (18:22). The appearance of Peter before the beginning of Jesus' instruction (17:24) and also at the end strongly suggests that the instruction on the priority of children and little ones is especially directed to Church teachers and authorities to remind them to keep this continually in mind in their ministry.

This last example is quite unusual. It is the case of someone with good intentions continually lapsing and coming back for forgiveness. It is typical of a child or "little one" who often acts and then reflects about it too late. Surely there should be a limit to human patience, as Peter suggests with his question. But no, God has no limits on his forgiveness and care for little ones: "Seventy times seven" means there can be no end to forgiveness and patience. The only limits God sets are that we must be willing to extend to others the same generous forgiveness that we have received ourselves. So the lord of the parable (representing God) says to the servant unwilling to forgive a minor debt of a fellow worker: "Should not you have had mercy on your fellow servant as I had mercy on you?" (18:33).

While Matthew's community discourse finishes in 19:1 with

a literary ending, he has, like Mark, another children's story to provide a literary frame for the initial reference to children in 18:1:

> Then children were brought to him that he might lay his hands on them and pray. The disciples rebuked the people but Jesus said, "Let the children come to me, and do not hinder them; for to such belongs the kingdom of heaven." And he laid his hands on them and went away (19:13-15).

Matthew does not have the adoption ritual with its blessing of children that we saw in Mark. However, he does have an emphasis of his own. He mentions twice, at the beginning and end, how Jesus laid his hands on the children, in the first case with an accompanying prayer. Matthew may have in mind the significance of laying on of hands in the early Church. This meant an empowering and transmission of authority. Matthew may be telling us in his own way that children have been especially chosen by Jesus to represent his own person and authority.

Matthew's central teachings on children/"little ones" continue in the rest of of his Gospel. First of all, he builds on the Old Testament wisdom / children theme that we discussed in Part I. Jesus emphasizes that the great wonders and wisdom of God are often hidden from the wise and prudent of this world and revealed to children: "At that time Jesus declared, 'I thank you, Father, Lord of heaven and earth, that you have hidden these things from the wise and understanding and revealed them to babes'" (11:25). When Jesus entered the Temple in Jerusalem for the last time, he contrasted the proud attitude of religious leaders and teachers to that of children who saw Jesus' wonderful deeds and exclaimed, "Hosanna to the Son of David" (21:15). When the scribes and Pharisees were indignant at these words, Jesus replied by quoting Psalm 8:2 which presents children as open to the wonders of God in the universe: Jesus said to them, "Have you never read, 'Out of

*also, only children could sing & not be arrested — see J. Fleming notes* the mouths of babes and sucklings you have brought perfect praise'?'' (21:16).

However, in Matthew's last judgment scene, we find a final emphasis on and summary of the theme of Jesus' identification with children and little ones who now include the hungry, thirsty, naked, strangers, prisoners, and sick. To make the teaching as forceful as possible, Matthew makes use of emphatic repetition. The identification with Jesus emerges powerfully with the repeated use of the pronouns ''I'' and ''me'': ''*I* was hungry and you gave *me* food, *I* was thirsty and you gave *me* drink, *I* was a stranger and you welcomed *me*, *I* was naked and you clothed *me*, *I* was sick and you visited *me*, *I* was in prison, and you came to *me* (25:35-36). In surprise, the righteous answer by repeating Jesus' words of identification with those in need: ''When did we see *you* hungry and feed *you* or thirsty and give *you* to drink? And when did we see *you* a stranger and welcome *you* or naked and clothe *you*? And when did we see *you* sick or in prison and visit *you*?'' (25:37-39).

The King and Judge then answers their questions by a solemn Amen statement that explicitly identifies him with these ''last or least'': ''Amen I say to you, as you did it to one of the least of these my brethren, you did it to me'' (25:40). To make this teaching as emphatic as possible, the whole scene is reenacted from a negative standpoint. Jesus sends away those on his left hand because they did *not* identify him with those who were hungry, thirsty, naked, strangers, sick, or in prison. They respond, like the just, asking when they saw Jesus and did not respond to him. Jesus then answers with a second Amen statement: ''Amen I say to you, as you did it not to one of the least of these, you did it not to me'' (25:45).

**Summary**

Matthew's infancy stories present Jesus as the chosen Child who identifies with his people and fulfills their expectations.

This prepares the way for his later presentation of the child as model for the believer. New in Matthew are the following themes: children become models of conversion and the virtue of humility; Jesus strongly identifies with them and emphasizes their importance. Children become models for Matthew's discourse on discipleship in the Church. He expands the image of children to include those "least and last" in the kingdom, especially sinners and those who are hungry and in need. Matthew also builds on the Old Testament Wisdom literature which teaches that God's gift of wisdom is given especially to children. Jesus' words in Matthew's final judgment scene emphatically teach his identification with the "least of his brethren" in the person of the hungry, thirsty, naked, strangers, sick, and prisoners.

# 3

# The Children's Paradox
# and the Divine Child in Luke

Only Luke's Gospel begins with a personal introduction: "In as much as many have undertaken to compile a narrative of the things which have been accomplished among us. . . ." Here the author's concern for Scripture fulfillment emerges with the words, "The things which have been accomplished among us." Yet this concern will not cause Luke to merely repeat what other writers have already considered. Instead, Luke's aim is to show that God's plan in Scripture has been accomplished in a surprising way that runs counter to ordinary human expectations.

Luke's way to show this is through unusual paradoxes regarding the ways people ordinarily look upon God or religion. The author often presents these as surprising contrasts that would make people laugh. One of his favorites was the extraordinary birth of a child to Abraham and Sarah in their old age, a child they called Isaac from the root "laughter." This was because both parents had laughed when God announced the coming birth to them. So when Isaac was born, Sarah exclaimed, "God has made laughter for me; everyone who hears will laugh over me" (Gen 21:6). Luke's description of the birth of John the Baptist to his mother Elizabeth in her old age invites us to recall the Scriptural stories of Sarah and Isaac.

To illustrate Luke's use of comic paradox in his two-volume work, his Gospel and Acts of the Apostles, I wrote a book entitled, *God Makes Me Laugh: A New Approach to Luke.*[23] One of the chapter titles is, "The Kingdom Is Child's Play." There I sketched how Luke's Gospel provides examples of the surprising fulfillment of Scripture through children. I will draw on that chapter here but add considerable new material.

## Luke's Christmas Story and the Triumph of a Child

There is nothing more familiar to Christians than the Christmas narrative in Lukan stories they have heard again and again as children. Perhaps adults do not appreciate them as much because they have progressively suppressed the child within who so spontaneously identified with these stories. Yet as adults, we can discover deeper, new levels of meaning if we understand and appreciate the scriptural background behind them. We will be surprised to discover that these accounts play an important role in a central theme: God's surprising design to work through the least and lowliest ones in the human family.

The first scriptural connection is found by comparing the choice of David, king of Israel, and the birth of his descendant, the child Jesus. Luke carefully notes this connection with David: the angel announces to Mary that a child will be born to whom God will give "the throne of his father David" (1:32). Key words in the description of Jesus' birth are its location in *Bethlehem, the city of David* (2:4). The angels announce Jesus' birth to the shepherds with the words, "For to you is born this day *in the city of David* a saviour who is Christ the Lord" (2:11).

The shepherd motif is also a key to the connections between Jesus and David. David himself was a shepherd (1 Sam 16:11), and God called him to shepherd his people Israel (2 Sam 5:2). The role of a shepherd is to nourish and feed his flock, which for David will now be the people of Israel. In doing so, David the king will share God's own shepherding role for his people. Isaiah the prophet described this: "He will feed his flock, he will gather the lambs in his arms, he will carry them in his bosom, and gently lead those that are with young (Isaiah 40:11). A favorite psalm in Jewish prayer has always been Psalm 23 with its words, "The Lord is my shepherd, I shall not want; he makes me lie down in green pastures" (Ps 23:1-2).

The image of God as a shepherd is a favorite in the Bible. The prophet Ezekiel contrasts human shepherds, seeking wool for themselves (and of course lamb chops!) to God caring for his sheep: "I myself will be the shepherd of my sheep, and I will make them lie down. . . . I will seek the lost, and I will bring back the strayed. . . . I will feed them in justice" (Ezek 34:15-16). Consequently, the promised Messiah will be like God the true shepherd and King David: "I will set over them one shepherd, my servant David, and he shall feed them; he shall feed them and be their shepherd" (Ezek 34:23).

In view of this scriptural background of God and the shepherd king, we find remarkable similarities between the finding of the soon-to-be anointed King David among shepherds and the discovery of the child Jesus by the shepherds of Bethlehem:

> God said to Samuel the prophet: I will send you to Jesse the Bethlehemite, for I have provided for myself a king among his sons. . . . You shall anoint for me him whom I name to you (1 Sam 16:1, 3).

In Luke's Christmas story we have striking parallels: Jesse is the father of David who is often mentioned by Luke (1:32; 2:4, 11). Bethlehem is emphasized in 2:4, 6, 11, 15. The story of David centers on his *anointing.* Regarding the child Jesus, the angels announce to the shepherds that a savior has been born who is Christ (meaning anointed one) the Lord (2:11). The designation of the child will be by God himself, just as the angels announce to the shepherds that a special sign, that

of the manger, will enable them to discover the chosen child
and anointed one.

In the David story, when Jesse hears that the prophet
Samuel is coming to his house to anoint a great leader, he prepares a feast with his seven sons sitting at table with him. These
seven sons, especially the oldest, impress Samuel by their stature, strength, and appearance; however, God tells Samuel
that he has not chosen one of them. Samuel then asks the
father if perchance there is anyone else. Jesse answers, "There
remains yet the youngest (literally, the "little one," *mikros* in
the Old Testament Greek) but behold he is keeping the sheep
(1 Sam 16:11).

Similarly, in Luke's nativity story, the true king is not found
among the mighty and strong; he is found among "little ones,"
the shepherds who were often, like David, children or youngsters. These lowly and little ones recognize the little one as the
true shepherd among them. The sign is that of the manger,
for he is lying in the animals' place of nourishment. In other
words, he will be the one to nourish and feed his people. This
sign of the manger appears connected with a prominent Scripture in the first words of the prophet Isaiah:

> Sons have I reared and brought up, but they have rebelled
> against me. The ox knows its owner, and the ass its master's
> manger: but Israel does not know, my people do not under-
> stand (1:2-3).

In this text, the donkey, traditionally the dumbest of
animals, knows very well where its source of nourishment is:
his master's manger. So also the people should know where
their own food will be: the child in the manger is to be the
shepherd king and nourishment of his people.

In presenting Jesus as a little one, found among the lowly
children shepherds, Luke introduces a theme that will be
prominent in his gospel: God chooses children and little ones

stand for all the lowly ones, the outcasts, and those in most need of a shepherd and leader.

## Luke's Wisdom Child

In Part I, we studied the scriptural Wisdom motif that wisdom is a gift of God granted even to children. Luke describes the child Jesus as a wonderful example of this gift of wisdom, combining the humanity and weakness of the child yet possessing God's wisdom to an extraordinary degree.

Luke has two short summaries of this Wisdom motif. The first is after the presentation of the child Jesus in the Temple forty days after his birth: "They [the parents] returned into Galilee, to their own city, Nazareth. And the child grew and became strong, filled with wisdom; and the favor of God was upon him" (2:39-40). In other words, this child did not just drop from heaven. He is a human child who actually keeps growing and becoming stronger. The second summary is after Jesus returns from the Temple at age twelve: "Jesus increased in wisdom and in stature (years) and in favor with God and man" (2:52). Here, the gift of wisdom keeps pace with physical growth through the years. He becomes older (or taller); his spiritual and physical gifts show he has God's favor as well as that of the people.

The first summary above refers to the wisdom present in the child at his birth. Luke writes, "She [Mary] gave birth to her first-born son and wrapped him in swaddling cloths, and laid him in a manger, because there was no place for them in the inn" (2:7). The specific mention of swaddling cloths has special meaning because Luke refers to them again as part of a sign: "This will be a sign for you: you will find a babe wrapped in swaddling cloths and lying in a manger" (2:12). Of course, every child was so wrapped in those days. This custom probably arose out of the feeling that the newborn child was fragile and that the winding cloths would keep the spine straight. In reference to the child Jesus, the use of the word seems to emphasize the fragile humanity of the child.

Yet even more seems to be involved in the sign of the swaddling cloths. It is likely that such a sign would have a scriptural background along with others in Luke's first chapters. It is unusual that one of the two rare scriptural passages about swaddling cloths has a Wisdom context: Speaking as a child, King Solomon declares that despite his very human birth as a child wrapped in swaddling clothes, God gave him wisdom, the greatest gift of his life. We quote the text again for reference:

> When I was born, I began to breathe the common air, and fell upon the kindred earth, and my first sound was a cry, like that of all. I was nursed with care in *swaddling cloths.* For no king has had a different beginning of existence; there is for all mankind one entrance into life, and a common departure (Wisdom 7:3-6).

Luke's reference to swaddling clothes, when we keep this scriptural text in mind, indicates that the child Jesus combined the most sublime gift of being "filled with wisdom" (2:40) with his utter humanity and weakness as a child.

The second wisdom summary follows the story of losing, then finding the twelve-year-old child Jesus in the Temple:

> After three days they found him in the temple, sitting among the teachers, listening to them and asking them questions; and all who heard him were amazed at his understanding and his answers (2:46-47).

The Temple area was the place where the great teachers of Israel assembled their disciples and taught them. The ability to ask searching questions was considered a special sign of wisdom. It is significant that the foremost teachers in Jerusalem recognize Jesus' wisdom. Later in the Gospel, Luke will draw special attention to Jesus' teaching in the Temple. The Gospel begins and ends in the Temple.

The rest of Luke's Temple story concerns even deeper levels of the Wisdom motif:

> When they [his parents] saw him they were astonished; and his mother said to him, "Son, why have you treated us so? Behold, your father and I have been looking for you anxiously." And he said to them, "How is it that you sought me? Did you not know that I must be in my Father's house?" And they did not understand the saying which he spoke to them (2:48-50).

We notice here how the child Jesus sharply contradicts his mother. She says, "*your* father and I have been looking for you anxiously." However, Jesus replies, "Did you not know that I must be in *my* Father's house." These words suggest that Jesus' gift of wisdom is part of a close inner and mysterious relationship with his Father, in contrast to his earthly parents, especially Joseph. The text then notes that Jesus' parents failed to understand the deep meaning in his statement. Later in his Gospel, Luke again brings in the theme of God's gift of wisdom bestowed on little ones. Jesus says,

> I thank you, Father, Lord of heaven and earth, that you have hidden these things from the wise and understanding and revealed them to babes; . . . All things have been delivered to me by my Father; and no one knows who the Son is except the Father, or who the Father is except the Son and any one to whom the Son chooses to reveal him (10:21-22).

### The Child in Other Lukan Themes

The continuation of the theme of the Child as bread and nourishment for the world is central. We have seen how the sign of the manger, following Isaiah, indicates that the child will be the source of nourishment, especially for shepherds and little ones ready to recognize him. In Luke, this auspicious beginning prepares the way for the Gospel climax at a post-resurrection meal-apparition where Jesus, disguised as a stranger, reveals himself in the breaking of bread: "When he was at table with them, he took the bread and blessed, and broke it, and gave it to them. And their eyes were opened and they recognized him; and he vanished from their sight" (24:30-31). Then at a following meal, Jesus appears to the eleven disciples and eats with them. Just as his swaddling clothes at the beginning affirm Jesus' humanity, so his actually taking fish and eating it assures them that he is real and human, not a ghost (24:36-43). While still at table, Jesus' last words of the Gospel affirm the universal mission of the Twelve, that "repentance for the forgiveness of sins should be preached in his name to all nations" (24:47).

Luke has been preparing for this final meal all through his Gospel. He emphasizes Jesus' meals not only with tax collectors, but also with Pharisees and other Jewish leaders. The description of the multiplication of loaves is very similar to the final recognition meal in the resurrection account: the details, "When the day began to wear away" (9:12), are the same as the Greek of 24:29. The words used to describe Jesus' actions in the two meals are almost the same: "taking the five loaves and the two fish he looked up to heaven, and blessed and broke them, and gave them to the disciples. . . ." (9:16; 24:30).

The Last Supper story also prepares the way for the final post-resurrection meals with the risen Jesus which are the climax of Luke's Gospel. At the Last Supper, the place of the Twelve is also prominent, mentioned more often than in the other Gospels (22:7, 14, 24, 30, 31). In addition, the link with children is carefully included. The model for those at Jesus' table is the child, or youngest: "Let the greatest among you become as the youngest, and the leader as one who serves" (22:26).

However, this Last Supper is not only a liturgical meal, but the model for a table of the Lord to be shared especially with strangers and the poor. This theme of hospitality appears in "welcome"

Luke's first pages in contrast to the lack of reception offered at Bethlehem to the child in the womb of his mother: "She laid him in a manger because there was no place for them in the inn" (2:7). In contrast, in the Gospel finale, the disciples beg the stranger to stay with them, offering him hospitality. Consequently, they recognize Jesus in the stranger when they break bread (24:28-31). *Emmaus*

Luke has prepared the way for this final hospitality motif. In the story of the multiplication of loaves and fishes, only this Gospel mentions concern that the crowds find not only meals but a place to stay (9:12). In Luke's version of the Lord's prayer, Jesus asks, "Give us *each day* our daily bread" (11:3). It is noteworthy that Luke uses the identical expression "each day" or "daily" in his second volume to describe the "daily" distribution of food to widows and those who are in need in the early Church (Acts 6:1). This suggests that the evangelist considers the tables of believers to be places where the needs of the widows and the poor are provided for. At these meals, following Jesus' instructions, the apostles and Christian leaders should serve at table, as if they were the youngest or servants (Acts 6:2; Luke 22:26).

### Children as the Model for Luke's Central Journey Narrative

As we have moved through the various Gospels, it is remarkable how we find a growing stress on the place and importance of children. Perhaps this is due to increased reflection on the centrality of this teaching of Jesus. Luke's Gospel has a central journey narrative where he includes most of the special material and stories only in his Gospel. He introduces this section by a story about children and ends it in the same way. He does this to highlight children as the models for all the new teachings on discipleship that he will present. For most of these insights, I am indebted to the fine study by Jerome Kodell.[24]

The opening narrative about children in Luke follows:

> An argument arose among them as to which of them was the
> greatest. But when Jesus perceived the thought of their hearts,
> he took a child and put him by his side, and said to them,
> ''Whoever receives this child in my name receives me, and
> whoever receives me receives him who sent me; for he who
> is least among you all is the one who is great'' (9:46-48).

At this point, only Luke has the saying that the one who
is least is the greatest. This is because the child as an example
of lowliness will be a central issue in the teachings of the ensu-
ing journey section. Luke's version has Jesus place the child
at his side, before the statement that whoever receives a child
receives him. This action places the child in much closer prox-
imity to him and reinforces the teaching that receiving a lowly
one is to receive Jesus. This second theme about receiving
others will also be prominent in the teachings that follow.

Luke likes to teach through pairs of opposites, and this is
how the teaching on children makes its greatest impact. The
first opposing pair are the disciples and the children, which
we previously saw. The second is John and the exorcist casting out devils in Jesus' name. John said to Jesus, ''Master, we
saw a man casting out demons in your name, and we forbade
him because he does not follow with us.'' But Jesus said, ''Do
not forbid him'' (9:49-50). This links with Jesus' words about
children in 18:16 where he tells his disciples not to hinder their
coming to him. The outsiders, like children, are the lowly ones
in the kingdom.

A second contrast relating to the children is that between
John and the Samaritans who were the lowest of the low as
far as the Jews were concerned. Jesus sent his disciples into
a Samaritan town where ''the people would not receive him
because his face was set toward Jerusalem'' (9:53). James and
John wanted to call down lightning from heaven to punish their
lack of hospitality, but Jesus ''turned and rebuked them''

(9:54-55). Here there is a question of *receiving* Jesus as in the children's story. When not received, the disciple is not to respond in kind. Jesus' rebuke of the disciples is exactly opposite to the disciples' *rebuke* of those who were bringing children to the Master (18:15).

Luke's closing story about children follows:

> Now they were bringing even infants to him that he might touch them; and when the disciples saw it, they rebuked them. But Jesus called them to him, saying, "Let the children come to me, and do not hinder them; for to such belongs the kingdom of God. Truly, I say to you, whoever does not receive the kingdom of God like a child shall not enter it (18:15-17).

Luke uses the word for infants or tiny children to further sharpen his contrasts. This concluding story focuses on imitating the attitude of children if people wish to enter the kingdom. Those entering the kingdom must do so with a lowly and humble attitude, a quality Luke will stress in the journey narrative. Once again, Luke will use pairs of opposites to connect the teaching on children with surrounding sections.

The first pair of opposites involves the Pharisee and the tax collector (18:9-14). This parable concerns those "who trusted in themselves that they were righteous and despised others" (18:9). This attitude is similar to that of James and John in regard to the Samaritans (9:54). The Pharisee "stood up" and compared himself to a tax collector also praying in the Temple, thanking God he was not like him (18:11). "Standing up" symbolizes standing apart with a haughty attitude toward others. It is the very opposite of "receiving the kingdom as a child" (18:17). "But the tax collector, standing far off, would not even lift up his eyes to heaven, but beat his breast, saying, "God be merciful to me a sinner!" (18:13). This is the lowly attitude of the least in the kingdom of whom children are the example (9:48). Jesus concludes the parable with the lesson, "I tell you, this man went down to his house justified rather than the other; for everyone who exalts himself will be humbled, but he who humbles himself will be exalted" (18:14).

To sum up: Luke may rightly be called "the Gospel of little children." The stories of Jesus' childhood prepare the way for central motifs in the rest of the Gospel. The scriptural background of these texts are the key for discovering Luke's deep insights. He takes the theme of God's reversal of human power and applies it to the child Jesus. He is the child, the descendant of David promised by Isaiah. God directed Samuel the prophet to find a "little one." To be the future king, the youngster David was shepherding the flocks with other children. In a similar manner, the promised Child is found in a humble setting among shepherds in David's city of Bethlehem.

This child is recognized by humble shepherds through the sign of the manger in Isaiah. His place in the feeding crib symbolizes he will be the shepherd and source of nourishment for his people. The childhood stories also anticipate and foreshadow central themes in the Gospel of Luke. The recognition of the child as source of nourishment in the manger prepares for the Gospel climax and recognition of Jesus in the breaking of bread. The hospitality motif at Jesus' birth leads to the end of the Gospel and the reception of the mysterious stranger by the two disciples on the way to Emmaus. The two Wisdom summaries in the childhood accounts direct us toward finding indications that Jesus is the promised Wisdom child of the Scriptures.

The central journey narrative in Luke's Gospel is the locus where most new material on discipleship is found. Stories about Jesus and children introduce and conclude this central section as a literary frame. Through the use of contrasting pairs, children illustrate central qualities of disciples, especially those of lowliness and the ability to receive "the least" in the kingdom.

# 4

# Jesus' Beloved Youngster
# in John's Gospel

In Mark, Matthew, and Luke, we found the child image to be a model for true discipleship. John's Gospel will go even further and present an actual person, the young beloved disciple of Jesus, not only as a model but as a successor to Jesus. Consequently, it will be important to discover the identity[25] and role of this person as well as the unique features of discipleship that he illustrates. This model will be at the heart of the fourth Gospel's message , whereas the child was only one model in the other Gospels, although a significant one.

Right from the beginning of the Gospel, God's plan to create "divine children" is very evident. The Gospel prologue announces that Jesus, the eternal Word of God, came down among his people and took human flesh. "To all who received him, he gave power to become *children* of God" (1:12). This does not mean "children" in the sense of an image or model, nor is it a matter of human birth by the ordinary means of "blood, or the will of the flesh or the will of man" (1:13). It is a whole new origin and mode of life that can only be expressed by the phrase "born . . . of God" (1:13).

How to become "born of God" is the central theme of the story of Nicodemus. This Jewish teacher came to Jesus by night and acknowledged him to be a teacher from God because of

his signs or miracles. Jesus answered him by moving away
from external signs to the necessity for a radical interior change:
"Amen, Amen, I say to you, unless one is born anew, he cannot enter the kingdom of God" (3:3). Nicodemus understood
this statement on a purely human plane and replied that it was
completely impossible: "How can a person be born again when
old? Can one enter a second time into a mother's womb and
be born?" (3:4). Jesus explained that this was a new divine birth
made possible only by the Spirit of God: "Amen, Amen, I say
to you, unless one is born of water and the Spirit, that person
cannot enter the kingdom of God" (3:5).

The Gospel confirms the above statement in a final scene
of divine rebirth when the risen Jesus first appears to his
gathered disciples. Jesus greets them, shows them his hands
and side, and then breathes upon them saying, "Receive the
Holy Spirit" (20:22). The atmosphere is one of rebirth in view
of the scriptural background of this scene. In the biblical story
of creation, God created man and woman by breathing into
their nostrils (Gen 2:7). Jesus is now a second Creator by
breathing into his disciples the promised Holy Spirit. Breath
and Spirit are closely connected, since the Bible associates
human origins with the life-giving breath of God.

The fourth Gospel presents a model of such a "divine child"
through an actual person, the author or authority behind this
document. We find him mentioned explicitly for the first time
at Jesus' Last Supper where he occupies a place of honor at
Jesus' bosom: "One of his disciples, whom Jesus loved, was
lying close to the breast of Jesus" (13:23). Even Peter asks him
to find out from Jesus the secret of the betrayer's identity
(13:24-25). The Beloved Disciple continues to faithfully follow
Jesus, even though Peter publicly denied his Master (18:17).
Alone of Jesus' disciples the Beloved Disciple stood by Jesus'
cross, where Jesus designated him to take his own place as
son of his mother Mary (19:25-27). After receiving the news

of the empty tomb, he ran along with Peter to the tomb, entered in, and was the first to believe even without an apparition of the risen Lord (20:8). In the apparition stories, he is the first to recognize the risen Lord through the miraculous draught of fish (21:7). Stories circulated that Jesus had promised him he would remain alive until he returned (21:23).

In view of the central place of this anonymous disciple it is important for us to investigate whatever clues we can find about his identity, role, and function in the fourth Gospel as a model for the ideal disciple and child of God. Some of the clues will immediately appear from the Gospel text; others are hidden in the sense that only those familiar with their scriptural background in the Old Testament are able to find them.

## Sources for The Beloved Disciple as a Child or Youngster and his Role

If tradition and art were a sole guide, there would be no question of the extreme youth of Jesus' Beloved Disciple. However, the Gospel itself must be the most reliable source, and here we find important though indirect indications. The last words of the Gospel refer to a reported saying of Jesus that the Beloved Disciple was to remain alive until Jesus' coming (21:22). The author notes, "The saying spread among the brethren that this disciple was not to die" (21:23). Then he corrects this idea by writing, "Jesus did not say to him that he was not to die, but, 'If it is my will that he remain until I come, what is that to you?'" (21:25). Nothing in the whole incident tells us anything definite about the age of the Beloved Disciple. However, the text strongly suggests that he was quite young at the time of Jesus' saying, since the Gospel as we have it now almost certainly goes back not earlier than the last part of the first century.

Another hint of the Beloved Disciple's youth appears in the Gospel's triple mention of him reclining at the bosom of Jesus at the Last Supper (13:23, 25; 21:20). This is obviously a place of distinction, of one who shares the secrets of Jesus, since the Beloved Disciple asks about the secret identity of Jesus' betrayer (13:23-26). However, the description of being at Jesus' bosom more easily fits someone quite young. The Bible uses the expression in regard to intimate relationships such as the wife, husband, or child of one's bosom (Deut 13:7; 28:54, 56; Ruth 4:16). It is interesting that in the Book of Ruth, taking a child into one's bosom is part of an adoption ritual.

In addition, the relationship of Jesus to the Beloved Disciple gives us further clues. Jesus often says that the relationship of the disciple to himself is like his own to the Father. The Gospel prologue concludes with the words, ''No one has ever seen God; the only Son, [''God'' in some texts] who is in the bosom of the Father, he has made him known'' (1:18). This would suggest that the Beloved Disciple is like a son/child in the bosom of Jesus, just as Jesus is the son/child in the bosom of his Father. Jesus thus learns his secrets from the Father, just as the Beloved Disciple learns who is the betrayer from his intimate relationship to Jesus.

To obtain more information about the Beloved Disciple's identity and role, we must first investigate the literary journey background of the Gospel of John in light of the Old Testament. After this, we can go on to further study of the actual texts in which he is mentioned. However, before we do this, we must briefly state the reasons why the Beloved Disciple is not John, the son of Zebedee and one of the Twelve, although this has been a traditional view.

### The Beloved Disciple:
### Not John, Son of Zebedee, One of the Twelve

Biblical scholars have brought forward the following reasons why the Beloved Disciple is not John the Apostle, Son of Zebedee:

*1. John and his brother James were from Galilee where Jesus first called them along with Peter and Andrew* (Matt 4:18-22; Mark 1:16-20; Luke 5:1-11). However, the Beloved Disciple seems to be from Judea. He makes his first explicit entry into the Gospel while Jesus is at his Last Supper in Jerusalem. He is well known there to the family of the high priest (18:15-17). This Gospel has much detailed description about Judea and Jerusalem but lacks this in regard to Galilee (4:1-42).

*2. The Beloved Disciple, the authority if not the author behind the fourth Gospel, has attitudes quite distinct from John, the son of Zebedee.* Jesus calls John and his brother, "sons of thunder," (Mark 3:17) perhaps because they wished to call down lightning on unreceptive Samaritans (Luke 9:53-54). In contrast, John's Gospel is sympathetic to Samaritans, especially in regard to the visit of Jesus to Samaria and his long dialogue with the Samaritan woman (4:1-42).

*3. In the other Gospels, James, John, and Peter are closely linked together, right from the time of their call.* Among them, Peter takes precedence. However, in the fourth Gospel, the opposite is often true: Peter even has to ask information from the Beloved Disciple at the Last Supper (13:21-26). The Beloved Disciple follows Jesus to the cross and never denies him, while Peter denies the Master three times. The Beloved Disciple precedes Peter to the empty tomb, even though Peter actually enters first. Yet the Beloved Disciple is the first to actually believe in Jesus' resurrection, even before Peter: "He saw and believed" (20:8). In the story of the miraculous catch of fish, the Beloved Disciple is the first to recognize the risen Lord (21:7).

Few scholars have devoted more research to the fourth Gospel than Raymond E. Brown. In contrast to his own earlier views[26] in the Anchor Bible Commentary, he later wrote the following in his book *The Community of the Beloved Disciple:*

> By setting the Beloved Disciple over against Peter . . . the Fourth Gospel gives the impression that he was an outsider to

the group of best-known disciples, a group that would have included John son of Zebedee. . . . The external late second-century evidence identifying the Beloved Disciple as John is a further step in a direction already visible in the New Testament itself, toward simplifying Christian Origins by reduction to the Twelve Apostles.[27]

## The Journey Structure of the Fourth Gospel: Key to a New Approach

Any key to the role of the Beloved Disciple must be found within the total literary and dramatic structure of this Gospel. Here we will argue that the journey of Jacob in Genesis, chapters 28–35 is a model for the Johannine journey of the Word/Jesus. We shall point out that this journey begins with the first disciples' call (1:35-45) and ends with Thomas' confession followed by Jesus' final blessing on those who do not see but believe (20:24-29).

First of all, we are drawn to investigate Jacob's journey as a model because Jesus refers to Jacob's ladder/dream (Gen 28:11-17) immediately before the marriage feast of Cana, the first Gospel sign (2:11). Jesus tells Nathaniel,

> Amen, Amen, I say to you, you will see heaven opened, and the angels of God ascending and descending upon the Son of Man (1:51).

Secondly, we should know why the journey of Jacob would be of such interest to the writer and his audience. It is because the Fourth Gospel has a view of Jesus different from the other Gospels. These latter describe Jesus' journey from Galilee to Jerusalem followed by his suffering, death, and resurrection. The Gospel of John, however, concentrates more on Jesus' "inner" journey, that of the LOGOS into the world and its return to the Father. The opening Gospel verses announce, "In the beginning was the WORD and the WORD was

God. . . . All things were made through him." This Word incarnates itself in Jesus: "And the word became flesh and dwelt among us" (1:14). At the end of Jesus' life, the incarnate Word returns to God. At the Last Supper, the writer notes, "Jesus, knowing that the Father had given all things into his hands, and that he had come from God and was going to God, rose from the supper" (13:3-4). In Jesus' last testament in chapters 14-16, he announces that he is returning to his "Father's house" (14:2) and describes how his disciples can also follow him there.

In John's Gospel, we still have Jesus' journey to the cross and death. However, it appears to be more like the "external" part of the journey, while the real "inner" part is the journey of the Logos into this world and then its return to God. In John's Gospel, the "external" journey, through the use of signs, is a way to enter into a relationship with the eternal Word acting in Jesus. Aptly, then, Jesus describes himself as a *way* to the Father (14:4-6).

For a pattern of the Logos' journey, the author would likely have picked a familiar scriptural one for his audience. The Greek-speaking Gospel would have known the Old Testament Greek Book of Wisdom. In that book, we find a description of Wisdom's journey through history. There, she worked as an inner guide to the great individuals of Hebrew history beginning with Adam and continuing to Moses (Wisdom 10:1-21). In the Book of Wisdom, the work of Wisdom is similar to that of the Logos. The author places them parallel: "You have made all things by your word and by your wisdom you have formed human beings. . . ." (Wisdom 9:1-2). Among the great figures in the journey of Wisdom through history is Jacob, the Father of Israel:

> Wisdom rescued from troubles those who served her. When a righteous man fled from his brother's wrath, she guided him on straight paths; she showed him the kingdom of God, and

gave him knowledge of angels (or holy things); she prospered him in his labors, and increased the fruit of his toil. When his oppressors were covetous, she stood by him and made him rich. She protected him from his enemies and kept him safe from those who lay in wait for him; in his arduous contest she gave him the victory, so that he might learn that godliness is more powerful than anything (Wisdom 10:9-12, RSV).

In this passage, we note the special emphasis on Jacob's dream: "Wisdom showed him the kingdom of God and gave him knowledge of holy things" (10:10).

We can now focus on the significant parallels between the journey of Jacob and the Johannine journey of Jesus/Word. First let us briefly summarize the background of Jacob's dream and journey. Jesus' reference to the angels of God ascending and descending comes from the story of Jacob's dream/vision at Bethel (Gen 28:12). This took place during a great crisis in the life of Jacob/Israel. He had deceived both his father and his brother Esau by pretending that he was the first-born son and fraudulently obtaining his father's last blessing. In hatred and frustration, Esau planned to kill Jacob. To save his own life, and to obtain a wife (and descendants to fulfill God's promises), his parents sent him away on a long, difficult journey to Mesopotamia. Jacob was very much alone, in danger of his life, and fearful he would not be able to find a wife and return to his home. On the way he stopped at a holy place, Bethel, to pray for the success of his journey. An answer came from God in the form of an unusual dream (Gen 28:10-22) to which Jesus refers in his reply to Nathaniel.

In the dream, God reveals himself to Jacob through the vision of a ladder going up to heaven. The angels of God are ascending (with his prayers) and descending with God's response and gifts. God assures Jacob that he will be with him on his journey and that he will have numerous descendants (hence find a wife) and return safely home. A central point is that Jacob/Israel sees the Lord at the top of the ladder (or perhaps beside him). This brings out Israel's special privilege as one who has seen the Lord (see also Gen 32:30-31 where Jacob says that he has seen God face to face). After the vision, Jacob goes safely on his journey and finds his future wives, Rachel and Leah. The happy ending of the first leg of the journey is their marriage feast (Gen 29:22), parallel to the marriage feast of Cana as the first stop in Jesus' journey.

The key words in the dream are God's promise and Jacob's response. God says to him, "the land on which you lie I will give to you and to your descendants" (Gen 28:13). Jacob replies with a vow:

> If God will be with me and will keep me in this way that I go, and will give me bread to eat and clothing to wear, so that I come again to my father's house in peace, then the LORD shall be my God (Gen 28:20-21, RSV).

With this background of Jacob's journey/dream in mind, we can list some significant parallels to the Johannine journey narrative. First of all, we note immediately the closing words of Jacob's vow, "The LORD shall be my God." They seem like a counterpart to the confession of Thomas near the end of the Gospel with the words, "My Lord and my God" (20:28).

Second, Jacob's vision contains the essential promise that God will accompany him on his journey. The heavens are opened so the angels as well as God can come down to him. God says, "Behold I am with you and will keep you wherever you go, and will not leave you until I have done that of which I have spoken to you" (28:15). With this assurance, Jacob concludes his vow with the words, "So that I may come again to my *father's house* in peace, and then the LORD shall be my God" (28:21). We note the similarity to the journey of the Logos in the Gospel and Jesus' return to his *father's house,* of which he speaks in his last testament to his disciples (14:1-2). Also,

Jacob calls the place *Bethel*, "the house of God," and the "gate of heaven" (Gen 28:17). This gate or door corresponds to the "opening of the heaven" that Jesus promised to Nathaniel (1:51). It is also linked to Jesus' description of himself as "the door" and as the way to the heavenly mansion (14:1-10).

The end of Jacob's journey is also very similar to the end of the journey of Jesus/Logos in the Fourth Gospel. After a long delay, Jacob finally fulfills his vow to return to Bethel where "God had revealed himself to him" (Gen 35:6). God also finishes his journey with Jacob and returns to heaven: "God went up from him in the place where he had spoken with him" (Gen 35:13-14). The words used in the Greek Old Testament Bible for "God went up" are *anēbē ho theos*. It is the same verb used by Jesus when he announces to Mary Magdalene, "I ascend, *anabainō*, to my Father and your Father, to my God and your God" (20:17). This ascension of God is especially emphasized by the Book of Jubilees in these words, "And he [God] finished speaking with him and went up from him and Jacob watched until he went up to heaven."[28]

This ascension logically takes place after Jesus' last words on earth to Thomas, immediately after he affirms that Jesus is God, *Theos* (20:28). Jesus then gives a final blessing that is especially addressed to the Gospel audience: "Blessed are those who have not seen and yet believe" (20:29b). This corresponds to God's final blessing to Jacob before leaving him: "God appeared to Jacob again, when he came from Paddan-aram, and blessed him" (Gen 35:9). The blessing takes the form of a new name, Israel instead of Jacob. Keeping in mind the popular Jewish-Hellenistic etymology of Israel as one who sees God (found forty times in Philo), the last blessing of Jacob in Genesis is similar to the theme of "seeing God" in Thomas' confession and Jesus' final blessing.

Third, some important events during Jacob's journey also resemble parts of the journey of Jesus in John's Gospel and may have influenced the author's selection of stories. The motivation for Jacob's journey comes from his mother's plan to provide a wife and descendants for her son (Gen 27:43-44). As a result of God's accompanying presence promised in the Bethel dream, Jacob finally arrives at Haran at the end of a long, thousand-mile journey. At Haran, God gives Jacob a first sign in the form of a "water miracle," a water miracle because the watering of Rachel's sheep is mentioned five times in the story as a result of Jacob's sudden and unexpected strength in removing the enormous stone from the top of the well (Gen 29:1-10). No doubt the event receives such attention from the writer because it is God's "arrangement" for the formative marriage that results in the people of Israel.

After witnessing this "miracle," Rachel, Jacob's future bride, runs to tell her father, Laban, who welcomes him into his home. A month afterward, Jacob agrees to work seven years to obtain Rachel as his wife. The wedding feast, *gamos,* LXX, with its free-flowing wine marks the end of this time (29:22). This marriage feast and the birth of children from both Rachel and Leah mark the success of the first part of Jacob's journey. Parallel to this, the first Gospel sign after Jesus' reference to Jacob's ladder is the marriage feast, *gamos,* at Cana, with its sign of water changed to wine (2:1-11).

Fourth, the "seeing of God" motif is quite evident in both journeys. During his dream/journey, Jacob's visions of God are high points. First, he sees the Lord by the ladder (Gen 28:13); then, after the wrestling with an angel, he calls the place Penuel, saying, "I have seen God face to face, and yet my life is preserved" (Gen 32:31). Later Jewish writings, avoiding such direct language in meetings with the deity, refer to Jacob as seeing the "glory of God." This language is used by the Targums to describe these encounters. While later than John's Gospel, they reflect a growing tendency to avoid direct mention of God. Thus the Fourth Gospel frequently uses the word "glory" for such encounters with the deity. The signs of Jesus in this Gospel are ways of experiencing the "glory of God" manifested in Jesus (2:11; 11:4, 40). The total experience is summed up in the words, "We saw his glory, glory as of the only Son from the Father" (1:14).

This "seeing of God" is intimately connected with the common Bethel/Temple theme at the beginning and end of the journeys of both Jacob and Jesus. In regard to Jacob, his journey begins with his mysterious arrival "at a certain place" (Gen 28:11). On awakening from his significant dream, Jacob exclaims, "Surely the LORD was in this place and I did not know it." In view of this divine presence, Jacob calls the place "Bethel, *the house of God*" (28:17, 19). Consequently, Jacob vows to build there a place of worship. He promises, "This stone which I have set up for a pillar shall be God's house," and adds that he will financially support worship there by saying," Of all you give me, I will give you tithes" (Gen 28:22).

At the end of Jacob's journey, God himself gave him the final order to return to Bethel to offer worship. He said to Jacob, "Arise, go up to Bethel, and dwell there; and make an altar to the God who appeared to you when you fled from your brother Esau" (Gen 35:1). In obedience to God and to fulfill his vow, Jacob returns to Bethel where he offers worship by setting up a sacred pillar and pouring drink offerings upon it (35:14). Once again, he names the place "Bethel, *the house of God*." Thus both the external journey of Jacob and the inner journey of the Word/Wisdom within Jacob begin and end at Bethel where God "goes up" to heaven just as Jacob "goes up" to Bethel (35:1, 13).

The Temple motif in Jacob's journey is also very evident in early extrabiblical literature where it may be connected to the hope that God will build a future Temple in the last times. The Book of Jubilees dwells at length on Jacob's worship at Bethel and his intention to build a temple there. Jubilees has

Jacob fulfill his promise to worship on that spot by describing how this took place at the feast of Tabernacles with Levi the priest offering sacrifices at Bethel.[29] Jacob also desired to build a temple in the same place: ''Jacob planned to build up that place and to build a wall around the court and to sanctify it and to make it eternally holy for himself and his sons after him.''

The Temple scroll of the Dead Sea Scrolls continues the emphasis on the connections between Jacob, the Temple, and Bethel in these words of God,

> I will consecrate my Temple by my glory on which I will settle my glory until the day of the blessing [or, in the day of creation] on which I will create my Temple and establish it for myself for all times according to the covenant which I have made with Jacob at Bethel.[30]

By way of comparison, we can now suggest that the journey of the Word in John's Gospel begins and ends with the same Temple theme, based on the model of the Jacob/Bethel journey. The Fourth Gospel begins with the summary prologue statement that Jesus became a Temple of the Word: ''The Word became flesh and pitched his tent among us'' (1:14). These words announce a journey motif. Yet Jesus' disciples will only know Jesus as the Temple of the Word after his resurrection.

This postresurrection knowledge is indicated by the writer immediately after the wedding at Cana in the story of Jesus' visit to Jerusalem and his cleansing of the Temple. The emphasis in the account is on the *Father's house* and on fulfilling the Scriptures, ''Zeal for your *house* will consume me'' (2:17). When the Jews ask Jesus for a supporting sign, he replies, ''Destroy this Temple and in three days I will raise it up'' (2:18-19). The Jews do not understand Jesus' answer, so the writer makes the significant remark,

> But he spoke of the temple of his body. When therefore he was raised from the dead, his disciples remembered that he had said

this; and they believed the Scripture and the word which Jesus had spoken (2:21-22).

In view of this body of Jesus/Temple theme, the journey of the Word begins after Jesus selects his disciples/companions for the journey. The selection of the last, Nathaniel, has special significance, since it is followed by Jesus' announcement of Jacob's ladder at Bethel and the angels of God ascending and descending upon the Son of Man (1:51). Philip finds Nathaniel and tells him he has found the one of whom Moses and the prophets had spoken. When Nathaniel expresses his disbelief, Philip invites him to see for himself by replying, "Come and see" (1:46). Nathaniel responds to the invitation and comes to see Jesus.

Jesus' words to the disciples/Gospel audience upon seeing Nathaniel come are very significant: "Behold a true Israelite in whom there is no guile" (1:47). We have already suggested that these words prepare for a central Johannine theme: that to come to Jesus and see him is to come to see the Father and that this all leads up to Thomas seeing Jesus and confessing him as his Lord and God.

This Temple theme is based on the common perception of the Israelite that coming to Jerusalem to worship is coming to "see God." This idea is found especially in the worship context of the Psalms. For example, the worshiper expresses an intense desire to dwell in the house of the LORD all the days of life "to behold the beauty of the LORD" (Psalm 27:4). Likewise, the pilgrim prays, "My soul thirsts for God. . . . When shall I come and behold the face of God?" (42:3). Again, "I have looked upon you in the sanctuary, beholding your power and glory" (63:3). Finally, "the God of gods will be seen in Zion" (84:8).

In the above texts we note the emphasis on *seeing*. This emphasis begins in the prologue, "We have *seen* his glory, glory as of the only begotten from the Father" (1:14). This seeing becomes possible, since Jesus dwells in the bosom of the Father and sees him, thus making it possible for him to reveal the Father to others even though no one thus far has seen God (1:18). This seeing motif is also found in Nathaniel's call; he is invited by Philip to "come and see" (1:46). Jesus tells him that a greater *seeing* will take place than Jesus' previous knowledge of Nathaniel under the fig tree. Jesus then refers to Jacob's vision at Bethel by telling him (and the disciples/audience) that they will *see* the angels of God ascending and descending on the Son of Man. This Temple/house of God theme at Bethel invites us to look further to see if Jesus will lead his disciples to a "seeing of God" similar to that of Jacob.

Especially within the resurrection stories, the writer seems to be carefully preparing for Thomas's final confession. There seems to be a gradual crescendo both in the use of the verb "to see" and the title, "Lord." Mary Magdalene reports to the disciples, "I have *seen* the Lord" (20:18). Then Jesus appears to the assembled group and "the disciples were glad when they *saw* the Lord" (20:20). Next the disciples tell Thomas, "We have *seen* the Lord" (20:25). Thomas, however, replies, "Unless I *see* the marks in his hands . . . I will not believe" (20:25). Finally, Thomas does see Jesus and exclaims, "My Lord and my God" (20:28). These words of Thomas are not just a credal statement but an act of worship using words addressed to God in Psalm 35:23. They do not result from the mere sight of Jesus' body which Thomas could identify by seeing and touching the wounds. They come from recognizing Jesus' body as a Temple and seeing God in him in the same way that pilgrims who came to worship at the Temple "saw God."

Jesus' journey seems parallel to the Jacob journey which began at Bethel, house of God, and ended with worship at the same spot. Added final elements may be the closed doors when Jesus appeared to the disciples and, later, also to Thomas (20:19, 26). This would contrast with Christ the door, (10:7) and the "door of heaven" at Bethel (Gen 28:17). In addition, the reference to the disciples being "inside" (20:26) may have a double meaning: the worship of Jesus in the house makes it truly a house of God, another Bethel.

With this closing in mind, the words of Jesus to his disciples/Gospel audience may have special additional meaning: "Behold a true Israelite in whom there is no guile" (1:47). To be "without guile" is among the qualifications for seeing God and dwelling in his holy Temple as expressed in Psalm 15:1-3 and 24:3-4 where the Psalmist answers the question, "Who shall sojourn in your tent? Who shall dwell on your holy hill?" This description paves the way for the theme of Jesus as God's holy Temple which will be brought out in the subsequent journey.

## Conclusion and Consequences

The Jewish Hellenistic image of Wisdom accompanying Jacob on his journey leads us to investigate whether the Fourth Gospel has used Jacob's journey as a literary and exegetical pattern. Jesus' own direct reference to Jacob's dream preceding the marriage feast at Cana points in this direction. Samples of significant parallels and areas of influence include Jacob's vow: "If God will be with me . . . and will give me bread to eat . . . so that I come again to my Father's house in peace . . . then the LORD will be my God" (Gen 28:20). Likewise, Thomas' confession, "My Lord and my God;" occurs before Jesus' last words and his return to his Father's house (14:2; 20:28-29). For Jacob, the heavens are opened and God comes down to be with him on his beginning journey; on his return, God went up, (*anēbē*) in Genesis 35:13 just as Jesus says "I ascend" *anabainō* (20:17). Especially important is the parallel Bethel/Temple and "seeing God" theme both in Jacob's journey and that of the Logos.

### Consequences of Our Search for the Identity of the Beloved Disciple

The literary parallels between the journey of Jacob with his twelve sons/successors and Jesus and his twelve disciples/ successors provide a valuable framework for discovering the identity and role of Jesus' Beloved Disciple. As we shall show in the next chapter, he is the beloved son and successor of Jesus and is parallel to Joseph as beloved son and successor of Jacob.

### The Beloved Disciple as Jesus' Successor and Son, Modeled on Joseph, Beloved Son and Successor of Jacob

We have presented Jacob's journey as a literary model for the journey of the Word/Jesus in the Fourth Gospel. Our next step is to examine this pattern more closely. As we do so, we will find another remarkable similarity. The journey of Jacob centers about the theme of succession: Jacob's marriage eventually makes possible the birth of his sons who become the twelve tribes of Israel/Jacob. Among these twelve, the Genesis narrative centers on Joseph, Jacob's beloved son. Joseph is the chosen instrument to insure the future of his family by rescuing them from hunger and bringing them into Egypt where they can have bread and life.

First of all, let us examine the succession theme. Jacob's journey concludes with his visit to Bethel to fulfill his vow. After that, the narrative prepares the way for the future by noting, "The sons of Jacob were twelve" (Gen 35:22). Then, they are all listed by name. After the death of Isaac, Jacob's father, there follows a genealogy of his descendants. Then the next journey of Jacob's descendants begins, a journey which centers about Joseph in chapters 37 to 50. The writer starts with the note, "This is the history of the family of Jacob" (37:2). Then, he tells his audience about Joseph, beginning from his youth in his father's house.

The Book of Genesis comes to a climactic point with the deathbed scene of Jacob, the patriarch and father of the twelve tribes. He makes his final testament and gives his last blessing to each of his sons who must carry on after him. Among the sons, Joseph is singled out for the most attention as well as an unusual abundance of blessings. In fact, the word "blessing" is not even used of the others, but it is used seven times in Genesis 49:25-26 as if to suggest that Joseph receives a sevenfold or fullness of God's blessing. Even before the final blessing, Joseph's special place is emphasized through Jacob's unusual gift of a mountain slope that he had acquired through a victory over the Amorites. Jacob says to Joseph, "I have given to you *rather than to your brothers* one mountain slope which I took from the hand of the Amorites with my sword and with my bow" (Gen 48:22).

Joseph's preeminence is further confirmed by the fact that Jacob adopts his two sons, Ephraim and Manasseh, as his own. The story is told in great detail (Gen 48:1-22). Jacob declares that his two grandsons will be his own just as Reuben and Simeon. He has the boys brought to him and places them on his knees in a ritual of adoption. He kisses and embraces them, then, one by one, places his hands on their heads to give them a special blessing. This means in effect that Joseph will have a double inheritance among the sons of Jacob and the tribes of Israel.

The final blessing and testament of Moses in Deuteronomy also witnesses to the special inheritance of Joseph. It starts with the words, "This is the blessing with which Moses the man of God blessed the children of Israel before his death" (Deut 33:1). Yet of all the sons of Jacob, Moses singles out Joseph for the greatest and longest praise and actually uses the word "blessing" only of him with the words, "Blessed by the LORD be his land" (Deut 33:13). He is also called "prince among his brothers" (Deut 33:16).

Second, the reason for Joseph's primacy will be especially important for us: he is the beloved son of Jacob, the offspring of his special love for Rachel. The author of Genesis notes:

> Now Israel loved Joseph more than any other of his children, because he was the son of his old age, and he made him a long robe with sleeves. But when his brothers saw that their father loved him more than all his brothers, they hated him (37:3-4).

In addition to this special love, Joseph is also described as being closer to God than the other brothers. He is gifted with God's secrets through dreams and divine revelations. One of his gifts, his ability to interpret dreams, is the means of saving the whole land of Egypt, and later the sons of Israel, from hunger and starvation (Genesis chapter 41 on Pharaoh's dream). The Bible often repeats that the Lord was with Joseph and showed him special favor (Gen 39:2, 5, 21, 23). The author, through the mouth of Pharaoh, praises Joseph: "Can we find such a man as this, in whom is the Spirit of God?" (Gen 41:38).

In extrabiblical literature, we find this same emphasis on Joseph as beloved son and successor of Jacob. In the Testament of the Twelve Patriarchs, we have these words in the testament of Joseph: "Listen to Joseph, the one beloved of Israel" (1:2) and "For my brothers know how much my father loved me" (10:5).

From what we have found out about Jacob's journey as a literary pattern for the journey of Jesus/Word in the Fourth Gospel and from the unusual place of Joseph as special successor and beloved son of Israel, we can see how the author of our Gospel could have found in the Old Testament a remarkable pattern for his presentation of the Beloved Disciple as successor of Jesus. We shall also see that the Beloved Disciple fits very well the image of an adopted son of Jesus. We must then turn to the Gospel itself to verify whether the author does in fact follow such a pattern.

Before we turn to the Gospel, we should note that Paul
Minear[31] has broken the ground for looking to the Old Testament for an understanding of the role and identity of the Beloved Disciple. Minear has made a special point that Benjamin
is called the ''Beloved of the Lord'' in Moses' last testament
in Deuteronomy 33:12. However, this is because Benjamin's
*land* is close to where the Temple will be built, and thus his
blessing follows that of Levi which is emphasized because of
his Temple priesthood. But there are a number of other ways[32]
in which Benjamin would not fit as a model for the Beloved
Disciple.

### The Disciple at the Lord's Bosom and the Joseph Model

First of all, the author's interest in Joseph would certainly
follow from his detailed use of the journey of Jacob and his
twelve successors as a model. The writer was surely aware that
Joseph was Jacob's beloved son and special successor. In addition, the Gospel has a specific reference to Joseph's unique
place: ''He [Jesus] came to a city of Samaria, called Sychar,
near the field that Jacob gave to his son Joseph'' (4:5). This
is a reference to the text we have already quoted from Genesis 48:22 where this land was given to Joseph as a special portion *more than his brothers.*

Here, however, we wish to argue from the text of the Fourth
Gospel that the references to the Beloved Disciple do in fact
point to his role as a successor and ''son'' almost independ-
ently of the background of Joseph in Jacob's journey. Yet if
we put both together, the image of the Beloved Disciple in
those roles is confirmed for the Gospel audience.

First of all, in the Bible, to be in someone's bosom describes
the most intimate of all human relationships. It is used of a
husband or wife (for example, Gen 16:5; Deut 13:6; 28:54, 56).
However, this closeness is especially true of a child in regard

to father or mother (for example, 2 Sam 12:3; 1 Kings 3:20; 17:19). It also has the connotation of a special place where secrets are kept (Job 31:33; Ps 89:51; Eccl 7:9). The familiar picture of Lazarus at the messianic banquet in the bosom of Abraham indicates the height of privileged sonship (Luke 16:22, 23). For our purposes, the ceremony of adoption by taking another's child into the bosom (or the lap) may be important in examining the significance of the image of the Beloved Disciple in Jesus' bosom (compare Ruth 4:16-17 where Naomi adopts Ruth's son by taking him into her bosom and making him her heir as well).

However, the essential matter is to discover the meaning of this phrase within the context of John, chapter 13. This chapter is part of a whole sequence, chapters 13 through 17, that are Jesus' last words and testament before his coming departure and death. It begins with a reference to his death, as the author notes that Jesus knew his hour had come to depart from this world (13:1). It is Jesus' final meal with his disciples. He washes their feet and tells them that they in the future must perform the same action for others: "I have given you an example, that you also should do as I have done to you" (13:15). The disciples will carry on Jesus' work to such an extent that those who receive them will receive Jesus himself: "He who receives any one whom I send receives me" (13:20).

During this final meal, Jesus' last discourse, his instructions to his disciples, takes place in chapters 14 through 17. Central in these chapters is the theme that although Jesus is going away, he and the Father will send the disciples a successor, the Paraclete, who will continue the presence of Jesus among his disciples (14:25-26; 15:26; 16:7-14). This emphasis on continuity and succession is so important that Jesus prays not only for his disciples but for future believers converted through his successors: "I do not pray for these only but also for those who believe in me through their word" (17:20).

Consequently, it is supremely important that the Beloved Disciple first appears designated at this time as the disciple "whom Jesus loved" (13:23). He has a special place at the side of Jesus during his last will and testament to his disciples. By this means, the writer wishes to show that the Beloved Disciple is a most important heir of Jesus. The interchange between Jesus, this disciple, and Peter during the Supper will show it.

Jesus carries within him the heavy secret that Judas, one of the Twelve is about to betray him. This matter is so crucial that it will set off the events leading to Jesus' saving death. This secret comes to the surface when the betrayer leaves the supper room under the control of Satan, and Jesus exclaims, "Now is the Son of man glorified" (13:31). When Jesus, "troubled in spirit," announces that one of them is about to betray him, the disciples look at one another, not knowing of whom he speaks (13:22). At this point, Simon Peter beckons to the Beloved Disciple lying at the bosom (*kolpos*) of Jesus and requests him to ask the master who it is (13:24). The disciple then leans on the chest (*stēthos*) of Jesus and finds out how Peter can identify the betrayer.

In this last statement, Jesus' greatest secret is given first to the Beloved Disciple. Even Peter, the rock, must request it through him. There is a parallel to this in the resurrection apparitions of chapter 21, possibly an appendix added to the Gospel. In the miraculous draught of fish, only the Beloved Disciple identifies the risen Jesus standing on the shore. He tells Peter that it is the Lord, and Peter depends on *hearing* this from him before he jumps into the water (21:7). Thus we see that "lying at the bosom of Jesus" at the Last Supper not only pictures an intimate relationship, but also carries the important meaning of the Beloved Disciple's sharing with Jesus his greatest secret and revealing it to others, even Peter.

From this, we can move further to investigate the nature of the Beloved Disciple's relationship to Jesus. The Gospel descriptions envision a type of father-son relationship modeled on that between Jesus and his own Father. First of all, there is a striking parallel in the beginning of the Gospel. Where Jesus is described as the only son dwelling in the bosom of the Father who makes him known to others: "No one has even seen God; the only Son, who is in the bosom of the Father, he has made him known" (1:18). The same revelation theme is also brought out in Jesus' statement, "The Father loves the Son and shows him all that he is doing" (5:20). Thus we have the combination of beloved Son and revelation in Jesus' relationship to the Father (compare also, 8:28; 14:10). Putting it all together, we would have the succession: God the Father—beloved Son Jesus—Beloved Disciple and son.

All of this is confirmed by Jesus' final testament on the cross to his own mother and to the Beloved Disciple. He tells her, "Woman, behold your son." Then he tells the disciple whom he loved, "Behold your mother" (19:26-27). The immediate context of this statement is just before the final events of Jesus' death which will be followed by an unusual flow of blood and water from the side of Jesus. The Beloved Disciple is a witness of this occurrence (no other male disciple is mentioned as present). The evangelist attaches special importance to this witness: "He who saw it has borne witness; his witness is true, and he knows that he tells the truth that you also may believe (19:35). Thus the Beloved Disciple is the person chosen to make known the meaning of Jesus' death to others. His witness is guaranteed by his position as favorite son and successor of Jesus, a place sealed by Jesus' final words entrusting the Beloved Disciple to his own mother as a son. Thus the son relationship was continued on through the person most closely associated to Jesus, his own mother.

## The Beloved Disciple As "Inner" Successor of Jesus

This thesis may be best illustrated through comparison with Peter. There is no question about the important place of Peter in this Gospel. He is singled out in the beginning when Jesus meets him, looks upon him, and gives him a new name in view of his special mission: "So you are Simon Son of John? You shall be called Cephas (which means Peter)" (1:42). It is Peter who makes a confession of faith for the others when many disciples leave Jesus because of his difficult saying about "eating his flesh" (6:66-68). On Easter morning, although the Beloved Disciple precedes Peter to the empty tomb, he does not enter first, but defers to Peter. After the resurrection, Jesus announces to Peter that he will continue his own shepherding role in regard to future believers (21:15-17). Peter's role seems to be more that of external successor and leader of the Twelve.

In contrast, the Beloved Disciple has more of an inner, understanding role. At the Last Supper, he is the first to know Jesus' greatest secret about his betrayal and coming death. He witnesses Jesus' death on the cross and points to the special scriptural meaning of the flow of watery blood from his side (19:34-37). At the empty tomb, he looks at the linen cloths and the rolled up sudarium and believes, whereas Peter does not as yet seem to understand that Jesus has risen (20:8-10). In the resurrection apparition, 21:7, it is the Beloved Disciple who recognizes the risen Lord, and Peter relies on hearing this from him.

This inner witness and succession of the Beloved Disciple is especially evident in the story of what seems to be his own call by Jesus (1:35-40). Although only Andrew is named as one of the two disciples, there are good reasons to believe that the Beloved Disciple was the other: the story contains Jesus' first words to disciples and thus parallels his last words to the Beloved Disciple at the foot of the cross in 19:27. The account is also in much greater detail than the others and seems to draw its source from personal reminiscences. Even the hour of the meeting is recalled (1:39).

In addition, the above encounter takes place after John the

Baptist had pointed out Jesus as the "Lamb of God who takes away the sins of the world" (1:36). Thus it parallels the witness of the Beloved Disciple at Jesus' death that the unusual events point to Jesus' fulfillment of the Scriptures about the eating of the paschal lamb and the sacrificial (flow of blood) nature of Jesus' death (19:34-37).

If this is indeed the call of the Beloved Disciple, the details would appear to be full of meaning in terms of his inner witness and mission:

> Jesus turned, and saw them following, and said to them, "What do you seek?" And they said to him, "Rabbi" (which means Teacher), where are you staying?" He said to them, "Come and see." And they came and saw where he was staying; and they stayed with him that day, for it was about the tenth hour (1:38-39).

A number of significant points can be drawn from this account. If it is indeed the tenth hour, about four o'clock, the disciples may very well have stayed overnight with Jesus in his temporary home. This is a special act of hospitality that could symbolize taking them into his own home or family. For the Beloved Disciple, it may have been the beginning of a relationship of adoption as a favorite son of Jesus. Secondly, there is special emphasis on the word "stay" or "abide" which is mentioned three times. This word "abide" has central importance in John's Gospel. John the Baptist had been told that he would receive a special sign: the Spirit would descend on God's Chosen One in the form of a dove and *abide* on him. It would show John the Baptist that Jesus is the one who baptizes with the Holy Spirit (1:32-34). Now Jesus, with this abiding Spirit, calls his disciples who abide with him and share his home. This may signify that they also share, or will share, the same abiding Spirit.

If the Beloved Disciple is an inner successor of Jesus in terms of divine presence and understanding of his mission, how does this relate to the texts about the Spirit in John 14-16 who is described as "another Paraclete," one who would be a successor of Jesus after his death? If we look at the texts describing the role of the Paraclete, we will find the same descriptions of the role the Beloved Disciple claims in the Gospel: the Paraclete is the Spirit of truth (14:16-17); the Beloved Disciple also proclaims the truth (19:35). The Paraclete bears witness as does the Beloved Disciple (15:26; 19:35). They both teach and remind his followers of what Jesus has said (14:26; 2:20-22). In this way, especially, the Beloved Disciple exemplifies the inner work of the Paraclete.[33]

## Summary

While the other Gospels present a child as a model or image of discipleship, the Fourth Gospel has an actual person, Jesus' Beloved Disciple. Both tradition and the Gospel itself strongly suggest that he was a decidedly young person. Internal evidence within the Gospel tells us that he was almost certainly not one of the Twelve. His identity and role can be found by examining the literary structure of the Fourth Gospel where a journey narrative is central to the total drama. This journey narrative is strikingly similar to the journey of Jacob in Genesis where God accompanies him by his presence and protection. In Jacob's journey, Joseph is his favorite son and his father's special successor because of their close love relationship. In this way he is a model for the Beloved Disciple. This disciple is prominent in the Last Supper succession narrative where, even in contrast to Peter, he reclines at Jesus' bosom and knows his inner secrets. He is the embodiment of Jesus' inner successor, the Paraclete or Holy Spirit, and is described in similar terms. He follows Jesus to the cross, even though Peter and the others desert their Master. He is the first person to believe in the resurrection without any accompanying signs and the first to recognize Jesus in his postresurrection apparition in chapter twenty-one.

Part III

# Epilogue:
# Finding the Divine Child

# Epilogue:
# Finding the Divine Child

"This will be a sign for you: you will find a child wrapped in swaddling clothes and lying in a manger" (Luke 2:12). In chapter three, we saw how this Scripture meant that the shepherds were to find beneath the appearance of an ordinary child the source of nourishment for the whole world. Since it is "the children's gospel," Luke probably had in mind a further meaning: Jesus, the Divine Child, is a model for his audience to look beneath the surface of "mere kids" and find the beauty and wonder of a divine child who can give new hope, life, and energy to what often appears to be a decaying world. In this brief epilogue we can only suggest a few directions for application of the biblical teaching on children. A bibliography will provide further avenues of study and application.

## 1. The Priority of Children in the Kingdom of God

When Jesus spoke about the kingdom, his disciples often had other, more self-centered priorities: "On the way they had discussed with one another who was the greatest" (Mark 9:34). When mothers brought their children to Jesus for his special blessing, the disciples rebuked them and tried to turn them away (Mark 10:13-14). We have seen the importance of these children's stories in the Gospels. They were repeated for special emphasis. Jesus, in no uncertain terms, rebuked his disciples and singled out children for his special attention.

Jesus gave priority to children because they were on the lowest rung of society and therefore the neediest. The image of a ladder helps us realize that without a sound bottom rung all climbing is dangerous and will eventually lead to failure. We must build from the bottom up if we want to form a just society. Rightly, then, the Gospels move from children to include the poor, the needy, the outcasts, and outsiders. The term "children" includes them all and prepares the way for them. The priority of children must be the byword and guiding force for all who wish to follow Jesus. "Children" include not only those who are physically children, but also the neglected child within all of us who must be given priority if we hope to make progress in personal growth.

## 2. Children of Death or Children of Life?

The Bible challenges us to make clear choices between life and death: "I have set before you life and death, blessing and curse; therefore choose life, that you and your descendants may live" (Deut 30:19). The priority of children is not an option but a choice between life and death. What happens when the children within or without us are unloved, bruised, or neglected? All too often their reaction is hatred or violence toward the persons or society that have mistreated them.

By way of application through the lessons of history, John Giannini has made the following observations:

> The frightening truth is that this Killer Child . . . plays in the larger political arenas. Richard Nixon, at the height of his success and headed for another term, sabotaged his presidency, the political life of many of his staff and cabinet, and resigned

the most powerful office in the world in disgrace. For his entire life, this tragic man has been trying to overcome the shame and guilt he felt as a child when he experienced his father's repeated business failures.

Adolf Hitler played out a similar tragedy on even a larger stage. A frustrated artist and battered in childhood by a sadistic father, he prophet-like, fanned the fires of hatred in a frustrated and demoralized people into a religious fervor that sought to create "a new humanity" and a "new order" under the swastika cross.

Finally, the United States, drawing on the innocent genius of Albert Einstein, through the ultimate differentiation, splitting the atom, brought into existence the first atomic bombs and dropped them on Hiroshima and Nagasaki. The crew of the bomber that dropped the bomb called it "Little Boy" and "Fat Boy;" and the survivors of the mob called it "The Original Child," a name of God.[34]

The matter of children's priority is not merely optional; it is a choice between life and death.

## 3. Children Are Our Best Teachers

I could choose no better way to illustrate that children are our best teachers than to quote from Ken Keyes' chapter on "Living Love With Children" in his book, *Handbook of Higher Consciousness:*[35]

> How do you use the experience of being with a child to aid you in your growth toward higher consciousness? The child can help you develop an awareness of what an "unfurnished" mind is like. When a child is first born, he does not chew over situations with his rational mind. He is just totally right here—right now. You can observe in a very young infant some (but definitely not all) of the characteristics of higher consciousness. . . . Your life will give you continual opportunities to show the child (and yourself) whether you are on a power level of consciousness or a love level of consciousness. Every glass of milk that

the child spills enables you to show him the world in which your conscious-awareness lives. Do you say (or even silently feel), *"I've told you a thousand times to be more careful."*
. . . When a child spills the milk, *you could welcome it as an opportunity to help both of you grow into higher consciousness.* You can say to yourself:
"The milk is spilled—right here, right now. Fussing about it won't unspill the milk. It will simply irritate both myself and the child. An upset child may unconsciously knock over another glass. . . . This is just a normal part of living. The immature muscle control of a child increases the probability of spilled milk. But even now as an adult I sometimes spill things. So we're losing a few ounces of milk, but that's absolutely no reason to lose our love and serenity."

## 4. Letting Children and the Child Within Us Play

One of our great modern tragedies is that adult life is being pushed more and more into childhood. Adult television shows and advertisements constantly bombard little children. More and more pressure is being placed on children to achieve academically even in their earliest years. All of this pressure curtails time for play that is the precious gift of children and the child within us. To be an adult does not mean to stop being a child; rather, it means to grow in responsibility while still allowing the child within us to grow, especially through play.

Jesus once taught by observing the children's games that he himself had played as a child. He said, "To what shall I compare this generation? It is like children sitting in the market places and calling to their playmates, 'We piped to you, and you did not dance; we wailed, and you did not mourn'" (Matt 11:16-17). Much has been written about the virtues of hard work and the "work ethic," but little has been said about the "play ethic." In his *Summa Theologiae*, Thomas Aquinas devotes special attention to a virtue he calls *Eutrapelia* (from the Greek root meaning "fun," "play," "recreation"). Here are some of Thomas Aquinas' observations:

> As bodily tiredness is eased by resting the body, so psychological tiredness is eased by resting the soul. As we have explained in discussing the feelings, pleasure is rest for the soul. And therefore the remedy for weariness of soul lies in slackening the tension of mental study and taking some pleasure. In Cassian's Conferences it is related of blessed John the Evangelist that when people were scandalized at finding him at play with his disciples, he requested one of his questioners who carried a bow to shoot an arrow. When this had been done several times, the man, on being asked whether he could keep on doing so continuously, replied that the bow would break. Whereupon the blessed John pointed the moral that so too, would the human spirit snap were it never unbent. These words and deeds in which nothing is sought beyond the soul's pleasure are called playful or humorous, and it is necessary to make use of them at times for solace of the soul. This is what Aristotle says, that in the social intercourse of this life a kind of rest is enjoyed in playing.[36]

Further on in the same discussion, Thomas answers the question, "Is too little playing sinful? His reply is very interesting, since our whole tendency is to ask whether too little *work* is sinful:

> Anything conflicting with reason in human actions is vicious. It is against reason for a person to be burdensome to others, by never showing himself agreeable to others or being a killjoy or wet blanket on their enjoyment. And so Seneca says, *"Bear yourself with wit lest you be regarded as sour or despised as dull."* Now those who lack playfulness are sinful, those who never say anything to make you smile, or are grumpy with those who do. Aristotle speaks of them as rough and boorish.[37]

Regaining the playfulness of a child does not mean merely playing games but rediscovering the ability to enjoy the pleas-

ures God has placed in this world. It also means the recovery
of a sense of wonder and the contemplation of all the beauties
of God's creation. The psalmist reminds us that children are
especially aware of these values: "O Lord, our Lord, how
majestic is your name in all the earth! You whose glory above
the heavens is chanted by the mouth of babes and infants"
(8:2-3).

A recovery of play in life does not mean we will be less effective in promoting justice and serving those in need. On the
contrary, it will give us new energy to share our happiness
with others instead of sharing our misery!

## 5. Finding the Original Divine Child

Just as the birth of the Divine Child in Christianity is the
paradigm for the birth of every child, so also in Hinduism de-
votion to Krishna as a child suffuses ordinary life with the divine presence. Elinor Gadon writes,

> In India there is a saying that there is no song without Krishna.
> The Divine Child Krishna, the adorable, mischievous God of
> the Hindus, is the fullness of love itself. Wherever he is present
> people are more loving—parents more tender with their chil-
> dren, children more affectionate with their parents. Lovers find
> the fulfillment of their desire. All of nature is in harmony with
> Krishna. The animals and the birds and the flowers, the trees
> and the hills sing his praises. Krishna is the grace of beauty and
> the wonder of joy.[38]

What are the obstacles toward recovery of this beautiful,
original, divine child within us? In the Gospels, we found that
Jesus' teaching on becoming a child implied breaking down
a process that often takes place in becoming adults: a harden-
ing and closure to change and a great hesitation to take risks.
Becoming a child means to reenter into the process of radical
change which implies openness and risk.

Brian Swimme, a writer and teacher at the Institute in Culture and Creation Spirituality in Oakland, California, writes,

> Though we have the unique opportunity of remaining in the creative emotional and intellectual flexibility of childhood throughout our lifetimes, we too can choose to or be forced to metamorphose into an "adult" rigidity. We take on the adult seriousness of cynicism, or resentment, or of racism; or we can throw over our divine inheritance as creatures destined to celebrate life and being and instead devote ourselves to the furniture in our houses; or we choose to dedicate ourselves to commercial enterprises whose true significance is the speed with which they transform earth beauty into junk heaps. But what is the result of this denial of who we truly are?[39]

The above author reminds his audience of the saying of the great philosopher Mencius in China: "The ultimate aim of all human education is to recapture the mind of the child." Also, Swimme recalls the story of Albert Einstein, whose custom at home gatherings was to immediately seek out the company of children. Once, a neighbor came to apologize that her daughter took up his time during visits to seek his help with homework. Einstein replied simply and honestly, "Your daughter could not have possibly learned as much from me as I have learned from her."

Swimme[40] examines the present attitude toward the education of children and sets it against the near-future and future advancements for the good of the world that could be brought about by children's liberation:

> At the present time we view educating children as a necessary evil. It would be better, we believe, if children came in as adults. Then we wouldn't have to waste any money on them. That's why we resent pleas for educational funding, especially concerning inner city schools. It's just such a bother. Education is something to get done with. The goal of the training process is to get the good job. . . .

Near future: We will realize that each child everywhere on Earth is the child of the Earth and requires tremendous care and nurturance if its powers are to be drawn forth. We will no longer pursue this task "for the economy" but rather because we will recognize quite simply the full potentiality of four billion years of life laden into each child. Our primary economic priority will be drawing forth this talent. Indeed, what we now spend for the military budget will be channeled into the work of drawing forth children. With the same energy we now use to scour the earth's surface in search of oil or precious metals, we will use in search of the talents and capabilities to be drawn forth from children.

Future: We will come to understand that all of human life is education. School and life identify because learning to become the children of Earth is an unceasing activity. Most importantly, we will come to see that *our greatest teachers in this are the children of all species.* All education will be understood as mutual: adults are to assist the children in developing their gifts; children are to assist the adults in their own healing and rebirthing as they enter a deeper region of childhood. And pervading this work will be the simple conviction that earth brought forth its eternally young species so that the universe as a whole might plunge into an incandescent celebration of the mystery of life and being.

## A Final Word to Parents

As a parent myself, I am acutely aware of how hard it is to raise children in our increasingly complex modern world with its unbelievable pressures on young people. This book is not meant to increase the burden of parents but to make them lighter. This lightening will come as we trust more and more in the inner resources of our children and on the largely untapped energy of the child within us.

Does the Gospel mean that we must change our ways of raising children? Much of the externals will remain the same.

Like a parent, Jesus shared his own wisdom with his disciples, and we will continue to give advice to children in the hope of sparing them from making hurtful mistakes. Yet Jesus' approach will always be a challenge to us, since he did not insist on laws, duties, and obligations but on invitation and grace. His central approach was to teach through stories and parables which embodied his own approach to life in the kingdom of God. In this way, he was grace and invitation in action. People felt free to respond to him and also *free to reject*. Even when he knew Peter and Judas would reject him, he put no pressure on them to change and repent. It is hard for us as parents to follow that model and resist taking coercive measures to make sure our children do not fail.

The New Testament way of forming disciples is to ask them to *follow* or *imitate*. Jesus' most important message to his disciples was "follow me." St. Paul used the same approach. He wrote to his Christians, "Be imitators of me, as I am of Christ" (1 Cor 11:1). The New Testament opposes all forms of mere human discipleship that rely only on obedience whether to teacher, leader, or parent. The work of a parent is to form disciples of Jesus, not faithful followers of themselves. Once again, "Come follow me" whether said by Jesus or by parents is a form of grace and invitation that allows room for rejection.

As we look back on our experience, the tendency is to regret lost opportunities and to wish we had acted differently to present a better model for our children. Yet we need to forgive ourselves, and as we do so we leave our children free to forgive us as well. Sometimes our models for being "successful" parents are based on the performance of our children at particular times. This standard can be deceptive and discouraging. This "successful" model might be likened to the performance of the elder son in Jesus' parable of the Prodigal Son. He was an obedient, hardworking, and faithful son who never got into trouble. He could truly say to his father, "These many years I have served you, and I never disobeyed your command'' (Luke 15:29).

On the other hand, the younger son was a typical "failure." He had spent all his family inheritance in loose, wild living. He had deserted not only his family but his country and his religious traditions by working for foreigners at the forbidden task of feeding pigs. Yet he had something precious within him that no one, nor any circumstance, could ever take away. In his most desperate moments he recalled the image of his loving parents, and this gave him the courage and hope to return home and start life anew (Luke 15:17-20). The words, "I will arise and go to my Father" seem to imply an inner resurrection of the original child within him.

*great!*

Indeed this image of the very particular love of someone, especially a parent, is the most powerful and irresistible force in the universe. It drew the boy back despite every obstacle in his path. His trust in that image was matched by his parents' trust in it also. This is symbolized in the parable by the father watching for him every day, seeing him from a distance, and even running out to meet and embrace him (Luke 15:20). This image of love, then, is the most precious inheritance that we can give to our children. They may temporarily lose everything else, but this love cannot be taken away; it will remain and unfold its power and energy when it is most needed.

# Notes

1. cf. bibliog.

2. James Dobson is the author of *The Strong Willed Child* and other books to which Anne Eggebroten refers on page 26 of her article.

3. quotation is from p. 26 of Eggebroten's article.

4. quotation is from p. 29 of Eggebroten's article.

5. Eggebroten, p. 27.

6. quotation is from Eggebroten, p. 28.

7. This section is drawn from my book, *Rediscovering the Impact of Jesus' Death: Clues from the Gospel Audience*, pp. 1–18. There I show how an understanding of Mark as dramatic narrative helps toward an understanding of the Gospel's impact on its audience.

8. Donald Senior's article surveys Mark's audience and Gospel from this standpoint.

9. cf. bibliog.

10. J. M. Derret's article provides a history of the interpretation of these stories and how their context and Old Testament background influences them. I have drawn on his study for the significance of the children's blessing in view of Old Testament models.

11. bibliog. pp. 128–133.

12. Via, p. 130.

13. A study of these similarities as well as a history of the interpretation of these Markan texts about the young man can be found in Fledderman's article.

14. This contrast is studied in detail in Jenkins' article.

15. It is taken from my paper presented at the 1989 Catholic Biblical Association meeting and submitted for publication.

16. Jenkins, esp. pp. 237–239.

17. Alter, p. 52.

18. Alter, p. 54.

19. Neyrey, pp. 433–434.

20. Couffrignal, pp. 645–646.

21. cf. bibliog.

22. For a more detailed picture of this situation, see my book, *Rediscovering the Impact of Jesus' Death*, pp. 19–48.

23. cf. bibliog.

24. cf. bibliog.

25. The material in this chapter about the identity and role of the Beloved Disciple in John is adapted from my book, *The Secret Identity and Role of Jesus' Beloved Disciple*.

26. pp. LXXXVII–XCVIII.

27. p. 34.

28. Jub 32:20.

29. Jub 32:3-7.

30. Col 29:8-10, translation from Y. Yadin, p. 113.

31. cf. bibliog.

32. The following are my reasons: Benjamin is given relatively little attention in Jacob's final blessing and testament. In Gen 49:27, Jacob merely states that "Benjamin is a ravenous wolf, in the morning devouring the prey, and at even dividing the spoil." This contrasts with the superabundant sevenfold blessing conferred on Joseph (Gen 49:22-26). Joseph also receives a double inheritance when Jacob adopts his two sons, Ephraim and Mannaseh, as his own. In addition, he receives a special portion of land in Sichem *more than his brothers* (Gen 48:22). In the final blessing of Moses, Minear compares the Beloved Disciple in Jesus' bosom to Benjamin who "makes his dwelling between his shoulders" (Deut 33:12). However, the reference makes better sense describing God as making his dwelling (in a territorial sense) in the hills (shoulders) of Benjamin where the Temple will later

be built. This priestly, Temple emphasis is evident in the special blessing to Levi which precedes that of Benjamin.

33. Alan Culpepper treats of the similarity of the work of the Paraclete and the Beloved Disciple in his book, *Anatomy of the Fourth Gospel*, pp. 123–124.

34. Gianinni, p. 35.

35. Keyes, pp. 143–145.

36. Summa Theologiae, 2a2ae q. 168.2.

37. Summa Theologiae, 2a2ae q. 168.4.

38. Gadon, pp. 25–26.

39. Swimme, p. 20.

40. Swimme, pp. 21, 46.

# Bibliography

Acquinas, Thomas, *Summa Theologiae*, trans., Thomas Gilby, (New York: McGraw-Hill; Blackfriars, 1972)

Alter, R., *The Art of Biblical Narrative* (New York: Basic Books, 1981)

Brown, R. E., *The Gospel According to John* (Garden City: Doubleday, 1966)

_____. *The Community of the Beloved Disciple* (Ramsey: Paulist, 1979)

Couffrignal, R., "Les femmes au tombeau et le jeune homme en blanc. Approches nouvelles de Marc xvi, 1-8," *Revue Thomiste* 87 (1987) 645-646

Culpepper, R. A., *Anatomy of the Fourth Gospel: A Study in Literary Design* (Philadelphia: Fortress, 1983)

Derrett, J. D. M., "Why Jesus Blessed the Children," (Mark 10:13-16 PAR) *Novum Testamentum* 25 (1983) 1-18

Fledderman, H., "The Flight of the Naked Young Man (Mark 14:51-52)," *Catholic Biblical Quarterly* 41 (1979) 412-18

Gadon, E., "Krishna: Divine Child of the Hindus," *Creation* 4 (1989) 25-26

Gianinni, J., "The Dynamic of the Wounded Child," *Creation* 4 (1989) 32-35

Grassi, J., *God Makes Me Laugh: A New Approach to Luke* (Wilmington: Glazier, 1986)

Grassi, J., *Rediscovering the Impact of Jesus' Death* (New York: Sheed and Ward, 1987)

_____. *The Hidden Heroes of the Gospels: Female Counterparts of Jesus* (Collegeville: The Liturgical Press, 1989)

Jenkins, A. K., "Young Man or Angel," *Expository Times* 94 (1981–82) 237–39

Keyes, K., Jr., *Handbook to Higher Consciousness,* 5th ed. (Berkeley: Living Love Publ., 1975)

Kodell, J., "Luke and the Children: The Beginning and End of the Great Interpolation (Luke 9:46-56; 18:9-23)" *Catholic Biblical Quarterly* 49 (1987) 415–30

Laverdiere, E., "It Was A Huge Stone," *Emmanuel* 92 (1986) 125–29

Minear, P., "The Beloved Disciple in the Gospel of John," *Novum Testamentum* 19 (1977) 85–98

Neyrey, J., "Jacob Traditions and The Interpretation of John 4:10-26)," *Catholic Biblical Quarterly* 41 (1979) 419–37

Senior, D., " 'With Swords and Clubs' - The Setting of Mark's Community and His Critique of Abusive Power," *Biblical Theology Bulletin* 17 (1987) 10–20

Swimme, B., "The New Cosmology," *Creation* 4 (1989) 19–21

Via, D. Jr., *The Ethics of Mark's Gospel—In the Middle of Time* (Philadelphia: Fortress, 1985)

Yadin, Y., *The Temple Scroll, The Hidden Scroll of the Dead Sea Sect* (New York: Pandora, 1985)

# Selective Bibliography on Children

Bettleheim, B., "Punishment Vs. Discipline," Atlantic Monthly, (November, 1985)

Chess, S., Thomas, A. and Birch, H. G., *Your Child Is A Person.* (New York: Norton, 1963)

Davis, B., and Wright, J., *The Magical Child Within You* (Berkeley: Celestial Arts, 1985)

Eggebroten, A., "Sparing The Rod: Biblical Discipline and Parental Discipleship," *The Other Side* 23 (1987) 26–37

Erikson, E., *Childhood and Society.* (New York: Norton, 1963)

Fraiberg, S., *The Magic Years.* (New York: Scribners, 1959)

Ginott, H., *Between Parent and Child* (New York: Macmillan, 1965)

Gordon, T., *Parent Effectiveness Training* (PET) (New York: New American Library, 1970)

Main, F., *Perfect Parenting and Other Myths.* (Minneapolis: Compcare Publications, 1986)

McGinnis, K. and F., *Parenting For Peace And Justice.* (Maryknoll: Orbis, 1981)

Miller, A., *Thou Shalt Not Be Aware: Society's Betrayal Of The Child.* (New York: New American Library, 1986)

————. *For Your Own Good.* (New York: Farrar, Straus, Giroux, 1983)